Joan West
2017

# Perspectives on the Hebrew Bible

## Essays in Honor of Walter J. Harrelson

edited by
**James L. Crenshaw**

MERCER
UNIVERSITY PRESS

ISBN 0-86554-330-5

*Perspectives on the Hebrew Bible:*
*Essays in Honor of Walter J. Harrelson*
Copyright © 1988
Mercer University Press
Macon GA 31207
All rights reserved
Printed in the United States of America

The paper used in this publication meets
the minimum requirements of American National Standard
for Information Sciences—Permanence of Paper
for Printed Library Materials, ANSI Z39.48-1984.
∞

*Library of Congress Cataloging-in-Publication Data*

Perspectives on the Hebrew Bible:
essays in honor of Walter J. Harrelson
edited by James L. Crenshaw.

120 p.     7 x 10″
ISBN 0-86554-330-5 (alk. paper)
1. Bible. O.T.—Criticism, interpretation, etc.   2. Harrelson,
Walter J.   I. Harrelson, Walter J.   II. Crenshaw. James L.
BS1192.P48 1988                                          88-39956
221.6—dc19                                                    CIP

# CONTENTS

Walter Harrelson:
  Scholar and Believer.................................................5
  **James L. Crenshaw,** *Duke University*

A Mother's Instruction
  to Her Son
  (Proverbs 31:1-9).................................................9
  **James L. Crenshaw,** *Duke University*

Solomon and the Origins
  of Wisdom in Israel ...............................................23
  **Ronald E. Clements,** *King's College*

Zelophehad's Daughters...............................................37
  **Katharine Doob Sakenfeld,** *Princeton Theological Seminary*

Religious Conversion
  and the Societal Origins
  of Ancient Israel.................................................49
  **Norman K. Gottwald,** *New York Theological Seminary*

The Redaction of Ezra 4-6:
  A Plea for
  a Theology of Scribes ............................................67
  **Hans H.-Mallau,** *Baptist Theological Seminary*

The Treatment of
  Earlier Biblical Themes
  in the Book of Daniel.............................................81
  **Rex A. Mason,** *Regent's Park College*

Double Literary Editions
  of Biblical Narratives and Reflections
  on Determining the Form
  to Be Translated..................................................101
  **Eugene Ulrich,** *University of Notre Dame*

# WALTER HARRELSON: SCHOLAR AND BELIEVER

Born 28 November 1919, in North Carolina, Walter Harrelson studied at Mars Hill College (1940-41), The University of North Carolina (A.B., 1947), Union Theological Seminary, New York (B.D., 1949; Th.D., 1953), The University of Basel, and Harvard University. He was Instructor in Philosophy at The University of North Carolina in 1947 and Instructor in Old Testament at Union in 1950. Between his study at Mars Hill College and The University of North Carolina, he served in the U.S. Navy (1941-45). After teaching at Andover Newton Theological School from 1951-55, he moved to The Divinity School, The University of Chicago (1955-60) and eventually to The Divinity School, Vanderbilt University (1960 to the present), serving distinguished terms as Dean at the last two institutions. His honors at Vanderbilt include, among others, the rank of Distinguished Professor, the Harvie Branscomb Distinguished Professor Award (1977-78) and the Thomas Jefferson Award (1985). He has been Executive Secretary (1967) and President (1971-72) of The Society of Biblical Literature, Rector of The Ecumenical Institute for Advanced Theological Studies, Jerusalem (1977-78, Spring 1978-79), and a member of the Revised Standard Version Translation Committee since 1976. His involvement in the councils of professional societies and the university is phenomenal, testifying to indefatigable energy, intellectual vigor, and high regard by others. His scholarly activity has been enhanced by a Fulbright Research Scholarship (1962-63), a National Endowment for the Humanities Grant (1970-71), and a Senior Fellowship from the latter granting agency (1983-84). From 1974-80 he served as editor of *Religious Studies Review*, one of several editorial tasks he has carried out with great care.

Walter Harrelson's publications cover a wide range of topics relating to the Hebrew Bible. His books include *Jeremiah: Prophet to the Nations* (1959), *Interpreting the Old Testament* (1964), *From Fertility Cult to Worship* (1969), and *The Ten Commandments and Human Rights* (1980). The scope of his interest becomes evident in a sampling of his articles for journals, books, dictionaries, and encyclopedias.

1. "Non-Royal Motifs in the Royal Eschatology," 147-65 in *Israel's Prophetic Heritage*, eds. Bernhard W. Anderson and Walter Harrelson (New York: Harper & Row, 1962).

2. "The Celebration of the Feast of Booths According to Zechariah XIV16-21," 88-96 in *Religions in Antiquity*, ed. Jacob Neusner (Leiden: E. J. Brill, 1968).

3. "The Significance of Cosmology in the Ancient Near East," 237-52 in *Translating and Understanding the Old Testament*, eds. Harry Thomas Frank and William L. Reed (Nashville: Abingdon, 1970).

4. "Worship," 1014-1018 in *Encyclopaedia Britannica," 19 (1973)*.

5. *"The Significance of 'Last Words' for Intertestamental Ethics," 203-13 in Essays in Old Testament Ethics*, eds. James L. Crenshaw and John T. Willis (New York: KTAV, 1973).

6. "Patient Love in the Testament of Joseph," 29-35 in *Studies on the Testament of Joseph*, ed. George W. E. Nickelsburg, Jr. (Missoula: Scholars Press, 1975).

7. "Famine in the Perspective of Biblical Judgments and Promises," 84-99 in *Lifeboat Ethics: Moral Dilemmas of World Hunger*, eds. George R. Lucas and Thomas W. Ogletree (New York: Harper & Row, 1976).

8. "Life, Faith, and the Emergence of Tradition," 11-30 in *Tradition and Theology in the Old Testament*, ed. Douglas A. Knight (Philadelphia: Fortress Press, 1977).

9. "The New American Bible," 139-51 in *The Word of God*, ed. Lloyd Bailey (Atlanta: John Knox Press, 1982).

10. "The Hebrew Bible and Modern Culture," 489-505 in *The Hebrew Bible and its Modern Interpreters*, ed. Douglas A. Knight and Gene M. Tucker (Philadelphia: Fortress Press, 1985).

11. "The Trial of the High Priest Joshua: Zechariah 3," 116-24 in *Eretz-Israel*, 16 (1982).

12. "Theological Education," 769-74 in *Encyclopedia of Religion in the South*, ed. Samuel S. Hill (Macon: Mercer University Press, 1984).[1]

---

[1]A complete bibliography of Walter Harrelson's publications will appear in *Justice and the Holy*, a Festschrift being edited by Doublas A. Knight and Peter Paris.

In his long and distinguished career Walter Harrelson has taught many students, most of whom were preparing for professional ministry. His vision of a just society, his boldness in criticizing prejudice, and his fight for a better world have captured their imaginations and through them have touched countless communities. Other students of his have followed their mentor, filling teaching positions in various colleges and universities. In him they found an imaginative and passionate thinker. I am one of those fortunate individuals, having studied with him from 1960-64 and having worked as his colleague from January 1970 through May 1987. My debt to him is great, my gratitude, boundless.

James L. Crenshaw
Duke University, The Divinity School

# A MOTHER'S INSTRUCTION TO HER SON (PROVERBS 31:1-9)

JAMES L. CRENSHAW
DUKE UNIVERSITY
DURHAM NC 27706

Two biblical proverbs mention mothers alongside fathers in the context of parental instruction. In each instance a gentle admonition is directed toward pupils, the probable meaning of the technical term $b^en\hat{\imath}$ (my son).[1] The first example, Prov 1:8, encourages the son to hear the father's corrective teaching ($m\hat{u}s\bar{a}r$), whereas the second, 6:20, varies the expression appreciably to "My son, guard your dad's command ($misw\bar{a}h$)." In this context the Hebrew verb $\check{s}m'$ has the nuance of obedience, an attentiveness resulting in specific action congruent with what the child hears. Both texts emphasize the weight of the father's instruction, which strikes the son as discipline and the interposition of an alien will. Both verses have the same statement about a mother's teaching ($t\hat{o}r\bar{a}h$), specifically "Do not forsake ($nt\check{s}$) your mother's teaching." The author of these admonitions could easily have composed anonymously parallel clauses to the one about the father; hence the references to mother throw light on the ancient educational context presupposed by these two sayings. The mention of father and mother implies that both parents taught their sons moral precepts.

The ideal wife and mother in Prov 31:10-31 alludes to this teaching role, although without stating who actually benefitted from her instruction. The

---

[1] Originally, the expression $b^en\hat{\imath}$ implied an actual father-son relationship. In time, perhaps through the intimacy of guilds, this word $b^en\hat{\imath}$ received broader usage, coming to denote a student who was not related by blood to the teacher, who concomitantly was addressed as $'\bar{a}b\hat{\imath}$, my father. The expression $b^en\hat{\imath}$ in Prov 1-9 has this technical meaning.

observation in 31:26 reads: "She opens her mouth with wisdom, and loyal teaching is on her tongue." That is, she speaks compassionately and wisely. The adjective *ḥesed* connotes steadfastness, an integrity generated by a deep sense of mutual responsibility. All three texts referring to maternal instruction prefer a single expression, *tôrāh*, and even this word is further qualified in 31:26 to focus on a mother's love. Here is no hint of harsh discipline, which arguably hovers over the expressions associated with a father's instruction.[2]

An ancient Sumerian text, The Instructions of Šuruppak, also refers to instruction from both parents.

> The word of your mother, as if it were the word of your god, do not ignore it. A mother is like the sun, she gives birth to mankind. A father . . . [his?] god shines. A father is [like] a god, his word is just. The instructions of an old man, may you pay attention to them.[3]

Like the Hebrew admonitions, this Sumerian one attaches a negative to the verb associated with maternal teaching (do not forsake, do not ignore) while reserving the unadorned verb for the context of paternal instruction (hear, guard, pay attention to).

Although Egyptian Instructions do not attribute teaching to mothers, these texts acknowledge their direct contribution to learning in other ways such as personally accompanying children to the place of instruction and preparing food for them to eat during their stay there.[4] This distancing of mothers from the actual learning process reaches its extreme form in Ankhsheshonq's observation that "Instructing a woman is like having a sack of sand whose side is split open."[5] Such a low opinion of women hardly left room for an astute mother to impart wise counsel. Nevertheless, this same author conceded that "A good woman of noble character is food that comes in time of hunger."[6] So the author did not subscribe to the view that all women were incapable of learning. Furthermore, Papyrus Insinger's perceptive insight that "No instruction can succeed if there is dislike"[7] opens the door for parental teaching, since affection for one's mother predisposed children to receive counsel

---

[2]The use of physical punishment to encourage boys who otherwise neglected their studies is widely documented, both in Egypt and in Mesopotamia.

[3]Bendt Alster, *Studies in Sumerian Proverbs* (Mesopotamia 3. Copenhagen: Akademisk Forlag, 1975) 137.

[4]Miriam Lichtheim, *Ancient Egyptian Literature*, II (Berkeley, Los Angeles, London: University of California Press, 1976) 141 (The Instruction of Any).

[5]Lichtheim, *Ancient Egyptian Literature*, III (Berkeley, Los Angeles, London; University of California Press, 1980) 170.

[6]Ibid., 178.

[7]Ibid., 192. The expression is sufficiently vague about the object of affection. It could be the subject matter, not the teacher.

from her. Thus it comes as no great surprise when The Satire of the Trades concludes the praise of the scribal profession with the following doxology: "Praise god for your father, your mother, who set you on the path of life!"[8]

A biblical text actually preserves a small sample of maternal teaching, but the instruction derives from no ordinary mother. This important remnant of a mother's *tŏrāh* comes from a Queen Mother (*gᵉbirāh*),[9] presumably a non-Israelite from the land of Massa in Transjordan. Her name is missing from Prov 31:1-9, but her son's name has survived in two forms, Lemuel and Lemoel. The probable meaning of the name is "Belonging to God," although "Lim is God" has been proposed on the basis of the Mari texts which refer to a god Lim.[10] A Minaean feminine appellation, Mawil (*mû'ēl*) has attracted attention as well.[11] The superscription to this mother's teaching identifies her son and recipient of instruction as a king. The text reads as follows:

> The words of Lemuel, King of Massa, with which
>     his mother instructed him.
> Listen, my son, and listen, son of my womb,
>     and listen, son of my vows.
> Do not give your power to women,
>     nor your sovereignty to women who destroy kings.
> Not to kings, Lemoel, not to kings—drinking wine,
>     nor to rulers—craving strong drink.
> Lest he drink and forget that which has been decreed,
>     and he pervert the justice pertaining to all the afflicted.
> Give strong drink to the perishing
>     and wine to those whose spirit is bitter.
> Let him drink and forget his poverty,
>     and let him not recall again his toil.
> Open your mouth for the speechless,
>     to defend at court all unfortunate ones.
> Open your mouth, judge fairly,
>     and defend the destitute. (Prov 31:1-9)

The literary genre, royal instruction, has left its mark on ancient wisdom, both in Mesopotamia and in Egypt. A Sumerian text "The Old Man and the Young Girl"[12] tells about a miserable old man who sought advice from the

---

[8]Lichtheim, *Ancient Egyptian Literature*, I (Berkeley, Los Angeles, London: University of California Press, 1975), 191.

[9]Israel's historiography credited various Queen Mothers with considerable influence at the court (2 Kgs 10:13; 1 Kgs 15:13; cf. Jer 13:18 and 29:2).

[10]A. Jirku, "Das n. pr. Lemu'el (Prov 31:1) und der Gott Lim," *ZAW* 66 (1954): 151.

[11]Berend Gemser, *Sprüche Salomos* (Tübingen: J. C. B. Mohr [Paul Siebeck] 1963) 107.

[12]Alster, *Studies in Sumerian Proverbs*, 92-94.

king, who first solicited counsel, then transmitted the suggestions to the old man as royal instruction in action. The counsellor's assessment of the situation was that the old man needed a young woman to invigorate him. Accordingly, the king spoke to a maiden and arranged a sexual liaison, probably a marriage. The text breaks off with the girl crying jubilantly: "Dance, dance, all young girls, rejoice!"[13] Although this text differs in form and content from actual royal instruction, it shows that Sumerians expected their king to possess unusual insight about human problems. The narrative also demonstrates the ambiguity of the relationship between ruler and sage, for advisors instructed kings, who in turn passed that wisdom along to others.

Egyptian royal instructions determine the actual characteristics of the genre. Only three have survived: The Instructions of Prince Hardjedef, Merikare, and Amenemhet I.[14] The first, a mere fragment, discusses marriage and death. The second advises Merikare in matters of statecraft, personal character, and religion. Emphasis falls on able officials, wise advisers, compassion, and providence. The third instruction tells the king's son, Sesostris I, how his father died at the hands of treacherous persons within the palace and suggests utmost caution. This advice reeks of cynicism resulting from experience.

A Babylonian text, Advice to a Prince,[15] differs in that it has omen form. The purpose of this text is to protect citizens of Nippur, Sippar, and Babylon from royal abuse of power, especially excessive taxation, corvée labor, and appropriation of their property. The omen form does not point an accusing finger at the king, but it solemnly announces the dire consequences of accepting bribes and participating in miscarriage of justice.

The close association of viziers and kings which surfaces in the early Sumerian fragment about the old man and the young woman eventually relaxed somewhat; as a result, these wise men transmitted valuable insights to their own sons and to the populace in general. Several Egyptian Instructions have survived which envision an audience other than royal sons: Kagemni, Ptahhotep, Any, Amenemope, Ankhsheshonq, and Papyrus Insinger.[16] An Aramaean text, Ahiqar,[17] enjoyed wide dissemination in the ancient world.

---

[13]Ibid., 94. E. Lipinski, "Ancient Types of Wisdom Literature in Biblical Narrative," *Isac Leo Seeligmann Volume*, Alexander Rofé and Yair Zakovitch, eds. (Jerusalem: E. Rubenstein's Publishing House, 1983) 39-55, writes that the king consulted a cloister-woman.

[14]Lichtheim, *Ancient Egyptian Literature*, I, 58-59, 97-109, 135-39.

[15]W. G. Lambert, *Babylonian Wisdom Literature* (Oxford: Clarendon Press, 1960) 110-115.

[16]Lichtheim, *Ancient Egyptian Literature*, I, 59-61 (Kagemni), 71-80 (Ptahhotep), II, 135-46 (Any), 146-63 (Amenemope), III, 159-84 (Ankhsheshonq) 184-217 (Insinger).

[17]James M. Lindenberger, *The Aramaic Proverbs of Ahiqar* (Baltimore and London: The Johns Hopkins University Press), 1983.

According to the story, this vizier to King Sennacherib instructed his adopted son, Nadin, who betrayed Ahiqar and caused him much suffering until circumstances required this vizier's service at the royal court and enabled Ahiqar to get revenge as well.

Unlike sentence literature, which expresses an idea in a brief statement, these Instructions often have long poems on a single theme. The same subject may extend over several paragraph units. Some topics occur more than once, and that also goes for popular proverbs. For example, The Instruction for Merikare cites the following proverb twice: "No river lets itself be hidden."[18] For the most part, the Instructions take up conventional themes such as the importance of eloquence, good manners, table etiquette, sexual decorum, wise administration, timing, integrity, sobriety, and self control.[19] These traditional subjects sometimes give way to wholly unexpected ones. The Instruction for Merikare includes a remarkable confession of wrongdoing.

> Lo, a shameful deed occurred in my time:
> The nome of This was ravaged;
> Though it happened through my doing,
> I learned it after it was done.
> There was retribution for what I had done. . . .
>
>
> Beware of it! A blow is repaid by its like,
> To every action there is a response.[20]

Perhaps more astonishingly, The Instruction of King Amenemhet I for his Son Sesostris I actually describes an uprising within the palace that cost the pharaoh his life.[21] The epilogue to The Instruction of Any stands alone among Instructions that have survived. Here Any's son, Khonshotep, responds to his father's teaching, objecting that the youth cannot possibly observe the moral precepts that come naturally to the father.

> The son, he understands little,
> When he recites the words in the books . . .
> A boy does not follow the moral instructions,
> Though the writings are on his tongue![22]

---

[18]Lichtheim, *Ancient Egyptian Literature*, I, 102 and 106.

[19]Michael V. Fox, "Ancient Egyptian Rhetoric," *RHETORICA* 1 (1983): 9-22, delineates five canons of Egyptian rhetoric: silence, restraint, gentleness, fluency, and truthfulness.

[20]Lichtheim, *Ancient Egyptian Literature*, I, 105.

[21]Ibid., 136-37.

[22]Lichtheim, *Ancient Egyptian Literature*, II, 144.

The father insists that people can change their dispositions, making the hard teachings easy to keep. As proof of this claim, Any points to wild animals whose nature has been changed—the fighting bull that becomes like a fattened ox, the savage lion that resembles a timid donkey, the horse, dog, monkey, goose—and to foreigners who learn to speak Egyptian. The example of the beasts fails to convince Khonshotep, who acknowledges that his father's "sayings are excellent, but doing them requires virtues."[23] Any responds that a crooked stick can be straightened into a noble's staff, or a straight stick can be made into a collar. Knonshotep's final appeal to an infant's nourishment is set aside by Any, who notes that older children require staple food.[24]

The biblical Instruction for Lemuel lacks any response on his part, but so do all other Instructions except Any. Lemuel's mother opens her teaching with rhetorical flourish,[25] then proceeds to warn her son about women, wine, and dereliction of duty. The Instruction consists of a superscription (31:1), a direct appeal to her son (31:2), and four words of counsel (31:3-9). The advice takes various forms: (1) an imperative with a negative (31:3), (2) counsel without a verb, but containing a rationale for the particular course of action (31:4-5); (3) a positively stated imperative with three accompanying jussives (31:6-7); and (4) three imperatives, positively stated (31:8-9).

*The Superscription.* Like the superscription to the sayings of Agur in Prov 30:1-14,[26] the Instruction for Lemuel has *dibrê* (words) rather than *mišlê* (proverbial sayings). The expression functions in 30:1 to focus attention on oracular revelation (although tongue-in-cheek), which was reinforced by the pun residing in *maśśā'* (burdensome oracle; Massa) and by the prophetic formula *ne'um* (whisper, oracle). Ordinarily accompanied by deity, here *ne'um* is governed by the word *haggeber* (the man). Although the superscriptions to several prophetic books have this word *dibrê*, it accurately describes what follows in Prov 31:2-9. The preferred word in Prov 1-9 is *mišlê*, perhaps *tōrôt* also. The genitive relationship in Prov 31:1 (words of Lemuel) is an objective one (words directed to Lemuel).

As the Massoretes have pointed the Hebrew text, the break comes at *melek* (king); one must translate: "The words of King Lemuel, an oracle with which his mother taught him." Because the word for king lacks an article, it is better to associate *maśśā'* with *melek* (king of Massa). According to Gen

---

[23]Ibid., 145.

[24]Ibid.

[25]One recalls the bombastic language of Prov 23:29, which also deals with the problem of excessive drinking. In this instance the question *lemî* occurs six times, wheras *mah* appears in Prov 31:2 only three times (assuming that *ûmeh* should be read as *ûmah*).

[26]See my essay entitled "Clanging Symbols," forthcoming in *Justice and the Holy*, Douglas A. Knight and Peter Paris, eds. (Philadelphia: Fortress Press).

25:14 and 1 Chr 1:30, the region of Massa was in Transjordan, hence North
Arabia. With the shift in the location of the *athnach*, <sup>ae</sup>*šer* now refers to *dibrê*
rather than *maśśā'*, in the sense of oracle. The resulting "with which his
mother instructed him" refers back to "words." The use of the verb *yiss<sup>e</sup>r-
attû* does not go well with *maśśā'* in the sense of prophetic oracle, which one
"proclaims" rather than "instructs."

*The Appeal.* The rhetorical flourish by which Lemuel's mother catches
her son's attention identifies him as very special. The threefold allusion to the
maternal bond moves from the simple Aramaic word[27] for son to the same
word qualified by "my womb," and finally to the same word qualified by
"my vows." Lemuel was special in the same way Samuel was, for he had
been given to Hannah as a result of divine solicitude, which evoked a promise
that the boy would be dedicated to divine service. For obvious reasons, the
paternal Instructions lack such amplification of the father-son relationship.
The bond between mother and child, powerfully different, enabled her to appeal to him in an effective manner. Her nurturing began before his birth, and
the care was spiritual as well as physical. That seems to be implied by the
reference to vows.

The threefold *mah* is variously interpreted. The Septuagint renders it as
an interrogative (what), but the Greek translator adds the clause "shall I say
to you, Lemuel my first born?" (see Isa 38:15). The Hebrew merely repeats
the interrogative "what?" On the basis of 1 Kgs 12:16 and Cant 8:4, the *mah*
has been rendered "Not." The first text uses the interrogative *mah* in parallelism with the negative, whereas its parallel in 2 Sam 20:1 has the negative
*'ên* instead of *mah*. Nevertheless, the meaning is the same whether one translates "What portion do we have in David?" or "We have no portion in David," given the sequel ("for we have no inheritance in the son of Jesse").
The verse in Canticles uses *mah* twice as a negative: "Do not awaken and do
not arouse love until it pleases." An alternative suggestion derives from Ar-
abic use of *mah* as a verb "to listen."[28] The verse thus yields, "Listen, my
son; listen, the son of my womb; and listen, the son of my vows." This reading accords with the appeals in other Instructions, where hearing is so important that one text, Ptahhotep, concludes with a lengthy discussion of this
topic.[29]

---

[27]An abundance of Aramaisms marks this instruction: *mah, b<sup>e</sup>rî, lamhôt, m<sup>e</sup>lākîn,* and *b<sup>e</sup>nê
h<sup>a</sup>lôp.*

[28]William McKane, *Proverbs* (Philadelphia: The Westminster Press,1970) 408-409 adopts
Eliezer ben Jehuda's suggestion in *JPOS* 1(1920-1921): 114. So does Otto Plöger, *Sprüche
Salomos (Proverbia)* (Neukirchen Vluyn: Neukirchener Verlag, 1984) 369.

[29]Lichtheim, *Ancient Egyptian Literature*, I, 73-74.

*The First Admonition.* The initial warning takes up a conventional theme in wisdom literature: do not become entangled in sexual relationships that may compromise you or sap your energy. It has been observed that this rather delicate subject is ordinarily the father's responsibility rather than the mother's.[30] The vocabulary of the admonition leaves room for ambiguity about the meaning of the advice. The noun *ḥêlekā* (your might) can also refer to material wealth, and Lemuel's mother may be warning her privileged son not to squander royal resources on women. The second half of the verse seems to advise against sexual liaisons with women of the harem who were favorably placed for plotting intrigue.[31] The unusual word *ûdᵉrākeykā* (and your nobility) need not be changed, inasmuch as the same usage occurs in Ugaritic literature. The Hebrew Bible probably has other instances of this meaning for the word *derek*, particularly Amos 8:14 ("Those who swear by Ashimah of Samaria and say, 'As your god lives, Oh Dan, and as the Sovereign lives, Oh Beersheba.'")

On the basis of Sir 47:19, which blames Solomon for laying his loins (*yᵉrekeykᵃ*) beside women, thereby subjecting himself to them, some interpreters emend the text to *yîrēkeykā* (Fichtner in BHS). Others opt for *dôdeykā*, which they translate in the same way (your loins).[32] The strange *lamḥôt* should probably read *lᵉmōḥôt* (to destroyers), not *lᵉlaḥᵃnôt* (to concubines), an emendation that has been suggested because of Dan 5:2. The final word (*mᵉlākîn*) may be Aramaic *malkîn* (counsellors); if so, the half verse refers to women's power to turn the minds of royal advisors from the important tasks of government. The verse appears to restrict itself to one subject, the threat posed by women. Alternatively, the second half verse warns against squandering royal energy on the battlefields, but such an interpretation lacks cogency.

*The Second Admonition.* Loose sexual conduct was frequently associated with excessive drinking, so the second admonition naturally covers this subject. Surprisingly, the main verb is missing, but the resulting emphasis on the two infinitive constructs achieves stunning rhetorical effect. As in verse 2 where the mother addresses her son, repetition occurs here too. There she re-

---

[30]W.O. E. Oesterley, *The Book of Proverbs* (London: Metheun Co. Ltd., 1929) 281. We do not know who assumed responsibility for instructing young boys in matters relating to the opposite sex.

[31]E. Lipinski, "Les 'voyantes des rois' en Prov XXXI, 3," *VT* 23 (1973): 246 thinks of visionaries. He translates: "Do not abandon your vitality to women, nor your ways to kings' visionaries."

[32]Plöger, *Sprüche Salomos (Proverbia)*, 371, refers to Dyserinck in this regard. So does D. G. Wildeboer, *Die Sprüche* (Freiburg, B., Leipzig und Tübingen. J. C. B. Mohr [Paul Siebeck] 1897) 90.

peats the Aramaic word *bar* (son) three times but avoids his actual name. Here in verse 4 she identifies her son, using the variant Lemoel, and repeats the phrase "not for kings," adding a parallel for good measure (rulers). A similar text in 2 Chr 26:18 throws light on the verbless *'al lamlākîm*. It reports that bold individuals opposed King Uzziah, saying to him: "Not for you, Uzziah, to offer incense to the Lord but for consecrated Aaronite priests" to do so. The context implies that the issue is one of appropriateness or propriety. Another text, Mic 3:1, reinforces this understanding of the grammatical form ("Is it not for you to know justice (*hᵃlô' lākem lāda'at 'et-hammišpaṭ*). Micah insists that the people's responsibility is to understand what justice requires of them. Here the sense of duty extends the weaker notion of appropriateness.

The prohibition of drinking, restricted to the ruling class, derives from an elevated view of kingship rather than from nomadic existence. Drinking wine and craving[33] something stronger interferes with the fundamental responsibility of nobility, the promoting of justice. Lemuel's mother may have left the verb unstated, but she clearly offers a rationale for her stringent counsel. The plural gives way to the singular, perhaps to focus the decision on her son alone ("Lest he drink and forget what has been decreed, and he pervert the arbitration of all the needy"). Ancient Near Eastern texts consistently stress the social obligations of kings to champion the cause of widows and orphans.[34] The Instruction of Šuruppak even brings together both concerns of Lemuel's mother, advising against judging when drinking. Both Merikare and Amenemhet I emphasize justice and compassion for the widow, the orphan, the poor, and the tearful.

*The Third Admonition.* With the well being of the destitute still in mind, Lemuel's mother suggests that her son can easily find worthy subjects for liquor and wine. The reversal in the order of these two drinks subtly underscores the harsh realities confronting those who are perishing. Their circumstances require strong medicine. Individuals whose lot, while odious, is nevertheless bearable can soothe their bitter spirit with wine. Again the personalized singular occurs: "Let him drink and forget his poverty, and let him remember his burdensome toil no longer.

In an intriguing section praising the creator, Papyrus Insinger remarks that god created wine to end affliction.[35] In addition, this text notes that wine,

---

[33]Instead of *'ēw*, I am reading *'awwē*.

[34]C. Fensham, "Widow, Orphan, and the Poor in Ancient Near Eastern Legal and Wisdom Literature," *JNES* 21 (1962): 129-39, reprinted in my *Studies in Ancient Israelite Wisdom* (New York: KTAV, 1976) 161-71.

[35]Lichtheim, *Ancient Egyptian Literature*, III, 210.

women, and food gladden the heart.[36] Within the Hebraic tradition, the exquisite praise of wine as strongest in 1 Esd 3:18-24 acknowledges its power to enable one to forget sorrow and debt. The text also highlights wine's leveling process, the erasing of sociological distinctions. In addition, the author recognizes the effect of wine on cognitive faculties. Kings, like subjects, succumb to its power.[37] It follows that kings who wish to rule wisely and to retain proper distance from their subjects so as to assure respect will avoid enslavement to wine.

*The Fourth Admonition.* The final admonition isolates instances of special vulnerability under the operative legal system and encourages the king to become a powerful and eloquent advocate for these people. A single verb ($p^e$-$tāḥ$) occurs twice in connection with royal advocacy, whereas two different verbs ($š^epaṭ$ and $dîn$) clarify the forensic aspect of this speech. Apparently, the word $l^e$ '$illēm$ (for the speechless) embraces actual dumbness as well as silence resulting from a disadvantaged social position.

Another reason for this concern on behalf of the speechless derives from the ease with which judges' decisions were influenced by bribes. Lemuel's role as spokesperson for the dumb is set within the larger context of arbitration for all those whom circumstances have overwhelmed ($b^enê$ $ḥalôp$). The exact meaning of this expression remains unclear. The decisive issue, whether or not the two classes of victims are synonymous, can not be ascertained. If the second group represents the same one as the speechless, the Nabataean expression $ḥlp$ $mwt$ may offer a clue about the meaning of $b^enê$ $ḥ^alôp$, perhaps persons overwhelmed by harsh reality.[38]

Other possibilities are "children of abandonment" (orphans) or "those who are perishing." Emendations have been proposed, two of which fit the context well ($b^enê$ $ḥōlî$, weaklings; $b^enê$ '$ālôp$, the powerless). The first assumes an error of sight, dittography of the letter *pe*, and the second presupposes a mistake of sound, the gutteral *ayin* replacing *ḥet*. The imperative $š^epāṭ$ governs an accusative $ṣedeq$ (equitably), while $dîn$ has a stock phrase as object, '$ānî$ $we$'$ebyôn$ (the poor and needy), which functions as hendiadys (the poor).

The Egyptian narrative, Protests of an Eloquent Peasant,[39] dramatizes the vulnerability of the lower class when unscrupulous officials forget the obli-

---

[36]Ibid., 199.

[37]I have discussed this text's rhetorical power in "The Contest of Darius' Guards," *Images of Man and God*, Burke O. Long, ed. (Sheffield: The Almond Press, 1981) 74-88, 119-20.

[38]McKane, *Proverbs*, 411-12.

[39]Lichtheim, *Ancient Egyptian Literature*, I, 169-84. Fox, "Ancient Egyptian Rhetoric," 16-18, contrasts the peasant's verbal virtuosity with the sages' canons of rhetoric ("The

gation to govern justly. In this account the peasant had the requisite persuasive ability to argue his case and to effect the redress of injustice. Not everyone
was so fortunate, and those who lacked a voice in the circles of influence lost
everything. The person who could effectively guarantee fair treatment of the
weak was, of course, the king. Lemuel's mother advises her son to open his
mouth to ensure justice for the speechless, not to imbibe intoxicating spirits.
The absence of motivation clauses in the mother's instruction is remarkable,
for this feature is typical of the genre. The tone of the advice to Lemuel suggests that his mother wished to instill in him a noble concept of kingship so
that responsibility rather than privilege would control his daily conduct.

This idealizing of kingship links up with a similar phenomenon throughout the ancient Near East.[40] In Egypt the pharaoh administered *maat* (truth,
order, justice) by creating cosmos rather than chaos, thereby establishing peace
in Upper and Lower Egypt. For this reason, he was looked upon as a shepherd[41]
and as a parent[42] who watched over the poor. His largesse extended to care
of widows and orphans, feeding the hungry, setting prisoners free, and cloth-
ing the naked. Because the pharaoh was god, he possessed understanding (*Sia*)
and authority (*Hu*). Nothing escaped his knowledge, not even thoughts, for
he tested the hearts of subjects. Normally, this wisdom was thought to have
been inherited, but Akhnaton insisted that the god revealed it to him in the
same way a teacher instructs a pupil.[43]

Various Mesopotamian kings claimed special favor from the god of wisdom. Hammurabi asserted that his wisdom had no rival; Ashurbanipal credited Nabu, the god of scribal wisdom, with the granting of wisdom; and
Nabonidus boasted: "I am wise, I am knowing, I can behold the hidden. . . .
The position in heaven of the New Moon, which Adapa composed, this work
I surpass, all wisdom is collected with me."[44] Even the king of the under-
world was thought to possess the symbol of kingship, namely the tablets of
wisdom.

---

most prominent characteristics of the peasant's style are repetitiveness, concatenations of ex-
travagant metaphors, and constant word-play.") Fox thinks this work may be a deliberate po-
lemic against wisdom's emphases on "restraint of anger, brevity of speech, avoidance of sharp
answers to superiors, and gentle speech" (17).

[40]Leonidas Kalugila, *The Wise King* (*CB*, Old Testament Series 15. Lund: C. W. K. Gle-
erup, 1980).

[41]D. Müller, "Der gute Hirte: Ein Beitrag zur Geschichte Ägyptischer Bildrede," *ZÄS*
86 (1961): 126-44.

[42]Thorkild Jacobsen, *The Treasures of Darkness* (New Haven: Yale University Press,
1976), traces the metaphors of deity in Mesopotamia from natural to royal, and ultimately to
parental ones.

[43]Kalugila, *The Wise King*, 30.

[44]Ibid., 59.

Ugaritic literature celebrates El's wisdom in the well known sentence: "Your decree, O El, is wise; your wisdom is everlasting, a life of good luck is your decree."[45] In another text Asherah observes: "You are great, O El, you are wise; your grey beard certainly instructs you."[46] Although this wisdom is restricted to the god El, human kings probably claimed a share of it. Azitawadda of Adana boasted that he had implemented justice, wisdom, and goodness of heart. Another Phoenician, Bar-Rakib, acknowledged that his father Panammu owned gold and silver because of his wisdom and righteousness. Here as elsewhere, a wise king took care of the poor, especially widows and orphans.[47]

Two Israelite kings, David and Solomon, are credited with wisdom. Neither David nor Solomon is remembered as championing the cause of the poor, although their judicial wisdom probably implies that.[48] The association of wisdom and wealth takes place with Solomon, for his primary interest was self-aggrandizement. This conduct earned him sharp rebuke for amassing horses, slaves, and precious metals, primarily gold and silver (Deut 17:14-17).[49] The king's failure to live up to the ideal eventually stirred disillusioned subjects to envision the birth of a royal child in whom virtue and knowledge would reside. The anticipated ruler in Isa 9:5 is endowed with the essential elements of royal protocol: wisdom, power, compassion, and well-being. Similarly, the ruler of Isa 11:2 has wisdom, understanding, counsel, might, and fear of the Lord. These qualities enable him to establish justice and peace.

Unlike the prophets, Israel's sages seem never to have challenged royal action directly, except for imaginary Egyptian rulers. Here the unknown author of Wis 6:1-11 warns those who exercise power over others that God requires a higher ethical standard from them than from ordinary people.[50] In addition, this author urges kings to receive wisdom from him so that they can stand close examination from the heavenly judge who shows deference to no one.

---

[45]Ibid., 62.

[46]Ibid. In a fascinating twist on this assumption that wisdom accompanies age, Santob de Carrión wrote that he dyed his hair not out of vanity but to keep people from expecting great insight from him. My friend and former colleague, Lou Silberman, tells me that the same sentiment occurs in rabbinic tradition. On Santob de Carrión, see T. A. Perry, *The Moral Proverbs of Santob de Carrión* (Princeton: Princeton University Press, 1987).

[47]Ibid., 65, 68.

[48]The brutal facts about their rule remained despite such attempts to paint the picture in rosy hues. Perhaps it is noteworthy that Solomon's wisdom is thought to have been a gift in youth rather than something he acquired through long experience.

[49]The repetition of the personal pronoun for himself (*lô*) stands out here and in the royal fiction of Eccles 1:4-8 (for myself, *lî*).

[50]Amos 3:2 makes a similar point.

An astonishing point of view surfaces in Prov 16:10 ("Divination is on the king's lips; in judgment his utterance does not err"). The idea that a king has direct access to the God's will and consequently renders accurate judicial decisions is at home in Egypt. As a matter of fact, this chapter in Proverbs contains several features that find their closest parallels in the land of the Nile. These include the notion of an abomination of the god (16:12), the idea that the royal throne is established on justice (*maat* = *ṣedāqāh*), the image of a messenger of death (16:14), and the belief that life resides in the king's face (16:15).

The other positive remarks in the Book of Proverbs about kings do not come close to these elevated observations. The acknowledgment that kings' special prerogative is to search out what God has hidden and the shrewd comment that no one can comprehend the royal mind stop short of celebrating a king's access to the deity's decrees (Prov 15:2-3). Likewise, the optimal assessment of a king's judicial acumen in 29:14 does not say that the throne was founded on justice, only that a dynasty that promotes justice will endure. This point is reinforced in 29:4, which mentions the stabilizing effect of royal justice on society.[51]

Israel's sages, like their counterparts in Egypt and in Mesopotamia, endeavored to maintain the status quo, for in that way they secured their own privileged position. This conservative stance was rooted in a firm conviction about the universe, which was sustained by an order deriving from its creator.[52] The task of maintaining the divinely ordained order was therefore an ethical and a religious duty, for which appropriate rewards accrued to favored individuals. Curiously, even after Israel's dogma of reward and punishment collapsed, no direct renunciation of kingship per se took place. Indeed, Qoheleth, the most severe critic of traditional wisdom, continued to foster the idealized notion of Solomon as quintessentially wise. At the same time, Qoheleth had some realistic assessments of royal weakness, both in character and in intelligence.[53] Nevertheless, these criticisms did not have royalty as their audience. Only Prov 31:1-9 falls into that category.

To what use were the other sapiential texts put in ancient Israel? Presumably, many early proverbial statements originated among the populace and functioned as a significant force in forming character. The attempt to ascribe

---

[51]Of the texts about kings and the court in Proverbs, only 22:21 seems to require a group of courtiers.

[52]Hans Heinrich Schmid, *Gerechtigkeit als Weltordnung* (BzhTh 40; Tübingen: J. C. B. Mohr [Paul Siebeck], 1968).

[53]The pertinent texts are examined in my commentary, *Ecclesiastes* (Philadelphia: The Westminster Press), 1987.

greater precision for particular collections has not garnered much support.[54] In any event, collected proverbs probably functioned differently from isolated truth statements. It is tempting to assume a pedagogic setting for collections of proverbs and instructions.[55] If accurate, this educational context even includes one royal instruction in its general teaching for young men who aspired to a scribal profession. Thus one mother's instruction for her royal son became teaching for a wider body of potential scholars. At the same time, Israel's sages receive the teachings of a foreign woman despite their own warnings about embracing the notorious *nokriyāh* or *'iššāh zārāh*.

---

[54]Udo Skladny, *Die ältesten Spruchsammlungen in Israel* (Göttingen: Vandenhoeck & Ruprecht, 1962). He thinks of 25-27 as a mirror for peasants and 28-29 as instructions for rulers.

[55]Even R. N. Whybray, "The Sage in the Israelite Royal Court," forthcoming in *The Sage in Israel and the Ancient Near East*, John G. Gammie and Leo G. Perdue, eds. (Winona Lake: Eisenbrauns) writes that "There is little doubt in my mind, on the other hand, that some parts of Proverbs, especially parts of chapters 1-9 and 22:17-24:22, were composed as 'textbooks' for young pupils—though not necessarily at a royal scribal school."

# SOLOMON
# AND THE ORIGINS
# OF WISDOM IN ISRAEL

RONALD E. CLEMENTS
KING'S COLLEGE
LONDON

The Old Testament is a literature which, even on the most conservative reckoning, has had a very complicated literary history. The traditional Rabbinic explanations of authorship[1] are clearly little more than convenient shorthand ascriptions which made use of the eminence, and hence inspired status, of the most prominent figures of the Old Testament: Moses, Samuel, David, Solomon and so forth. In part such ascriptions are related to significant aspects of the text, and in other respects they are little more than reflections of the assumption that inspired literature must have been composed by the most truly inspired persons. The extent to which these assumptions regarding authorship provide helpful and important guidelines to the way in which the literature is to be interpreted varies greatly. It is a matter of significance that the Pentateuch is ascribed to Moses, whereas it hardly matters at all to the understanding of the books of 1 and 2 Samuel that they have been ascribed to Samuel's authorship, at least up to the point of his death.

Over against this we can note that there remains considerable divergence of opinion whether the heading *leᵈdawid* for a large number of the Psalms provides any worthwhile information concerning how they originated or were

---

[1]The main passage dealing with such questions of authorship is to be found in *Baba Bathra* 14ᵇ; cf. S. R. Driver, *Introduction to the Literature of the Old Testament*, 9th ed. (Edinburgh: 1913) viff.

used.[2] At one extreme it is argued that the heading represents no more than a late assumption concerning Davidic authorship;[3] the other extreme is the argument that it indicates something important about the origin of such psalms in the Jerusalem cultus, or even reveals a direct connection with the Davidic dynasty of kings and their role in the cultus.[4] Certainly there is a widespread tendency among scholars to argue that the ascription of two major wisdom books of the Old Testament, Proverbs and Ecclesiastes (Prov 1:1; Eccl 1:1), does reflect something important concerning the wisdom tradition of ancient Israel. Whether the same is true of the Song of Songs remains an essentially different matter.

The author of Ecclesiastes has, according to a widely accepted scholarly observation, used the notion of Solomonic authorship to explore the literary and didactic potential of such a claim in Eccl 1:12-2:26. By drawing upon certain images of the wealth, success and indulgence of this celebrated figure of Israel's past, the author has contrived to express his verdict upon the value of such attainments. In any case both here, and almost certainly also in the ascriptions of the composition and collecting of wisdom sayings in Prov 1:1 and 25:1, the claim to Solomonic authorship rests upon the established narrative traditions regarding Solomon's wisdom to be found in the book of 1 Kings. We may take it as a useful working hypothesis, therefore, that the narrative traditions concerning Solomon's reign contained in 1 Kings, together with the short summarizing appraisals of Solomon's wisdom which relate closely to these narratives, form the basis for the claim that Solomon himself was the "author" of many proverbs and thus effectively the patron of wisdom in Israel.

Before investigating these traditions more closely, we may pause to reflect upon the general fact that it is not at all clear that wisdom needed a specifically identifiable "author" any more than psalmody required a David, or the law required a Moses. A fundamental axiom of the way H. Gunkel sought to trace the historical origins of Israelite literature was that *Gattungen* such as psalms, didactic sayings, riddles, work-songs and legal formulations be-

---

[2]The question of the significance of the ascription of many Psalms to David is dealt with by C. F. Barth, *An Introduction to the Psalms,* Eng. tr. R. A. Wilson (Oxford: 1966) 61-65; cf. further I. Engnell, *Critical Essays on the Old Testament,* Eng. tr. J. T. Willis (London: 1970) 68-122. Engnell sees such a title as indicative of the use of such Psalms by the king in Israel's royal ritual (so especially 77ff.).

[3]Cf. R. H. Pfeiffer, *Introduction to the Old Testament* (London: 1948) 645: "This brief title is purely conventional, and does not characterize the contents."

[4]Besides the writing of I. Engnell, cited in note 2 above, cf. also A. Bentzen, *Introduction to the Old Testament* (Copenhagen: 1952) 2:169 (also 1:147f.).

longed to specific activities and needs in society.[5] Their real authors were the people who used them and worked with them, not great figures of heroic proportions who were less caught up in the activities where such pronouncements and poems were composed. It was then largely a literary and fictional embellishment to credit the authorship of highly intriguing riddles, or spiritually edifying hymns, to specific personages. Furthermore it is usually in the nature of such compositions that they possess a relatively timeless quality, and are not rooted in the personal biographies of individuals. This is, in any case, largely something that we can readily observe in looking at the contents of such sayings and pronouncements. For the most part the proverbs and admonitions of the wise men of ancient Israel have little to gain or lose by being ascribed to Solomon. They are intended to be true and memorable in themselves, rather than on account of their notable authorship.

Bearing these considerations in mind we can look more closely at the traditions regarding Solomon's skill as a teacher of wisdom and a composer of proverbial sayings in 1 Kings and proceed to investigate what scholars have made of them. There are essentially two narrative traditions which relate directly to Solomon's wisdom, the first concerning his revelatory dream encounter with God at Gibeon when he went there to offer sacrifice (1 Kgs 3:3-15). This is inseparably related to the story of his discerning judgment in the case of the two harlots who each lay claim to the same child (1 Kgs 3:16-28). This is obviously intended to serve as a sequel to the dream encounter since it demonstrates that God had indeed endowed Solomon with immense human discernment.[6] The kind of wisdom that is credited to Solomon in this story is the insight into the hidden motives that lie behind a person's public posturing and claims which made Solomon a good judge in handling difficult cases. Such questions over joint claims of ownership where only one could be upheld are presented as being notoriously difficult to sort out in the legal traditions of the Old Testament (see Exod 22:7-13; Lev 6:1-7). The story ascribes to Solomon therefore a specific skill in juridical wisdom which made him a good and fair administrator. We can also wholly endorse the literary classification of this narrative, or combination of narratives, made by S. Herrmann as that of the "royal tale" (German *Königsnovelle*).[7] It is the kind of story that was told in order to support and embellish the claims of the monarchy,

---

[5]H. Gunkel, *Die Israelitische Literatur* (Die Kultur der Gegenwart, ed. P. Hinneberg) (Berlin-Leipzig: 1906) 90.

[6]Cf. M. Noth, "Die Bewährung von Salomos " 'göttliche Weisheit,' " *VT Sup* 3 (1955): 225-37; G. H. Jones, *1 & 2 Kings, New Century Bible* (Grand Rapids: 1984) 121ff.

[7]S. Herrmann, "Die Königsnovelle in Ägypten und in Israel," *WZ Leipzig* 3 (1953-4): 1, 51-62, ( = *Gesammelte Studien zur Geschichte und Theologie des AT*, TBü, 75 (Munich: 1986) 120-144).

particularly in this case in respect of royal interference in, not to say the complete takeover of, the administration of justice.

The second of the stories regarding the wisdom of Solomon is found in 1 Kgs 10:1-13 and deals with the visit of the Queen of Sheba. The center of attention of the story is the great wealth and opulence of Solomon's court (especially vv 4,7). This is a tale of wisdom and prosperity, so that, although the royal insight into what lay hidden in the queen's mind (vv 2-3) has subsequently become the subject of considerable romantic and imaginative expansion,[8] the story does not relate the practice of wisdom to any specific function or institution of Israelite society. Wisdom is the path to prosperity, and it would appear that the trading links between Israel and the Horn of Africa form the essential historical foundation of the story.[9] In this case the tale is told in emphatic praise of Solomon to show that Solomon was more prosperous and successful than any other of Israel's kings, before or afterwards. A summary judgment to this effect is then placed in 1 Kgs 10:23-25; "Thus King Solomon excelled all the kings of the earth in riches and in wisdom" (1 Kgs 10:23). This piece of good news is put first, since the bad news comes soon after in 1 Kings 11-12 with its accounts of disaffection, rebellion and eventual disruption of the kingdom.

In between these two stories concerning Solomon's wisdom is a comprehensive summary in 1 Kgs 4:29-34 that reaffirms the fact of Solomon's great wisdom and contains significant additional items of information concerning it. The location of the summary immediately following the list of Solomon's principal officials and his twelve district officers set over all Israel (1 Kgs 4:1-19) may also be regarded as of significance.

We may here consider some of the ways in which scholars have sought to pin-point one or other of the incidental elements of the tradition about Solomon's wisdom in an effort to uncover the historical roots of the tradition that he was a supremely wise man. Most to the fore here we should place the valuable and suggestive essay from A. Alt[10] which focuses chiefly upon the information contained in 1 Kgs 4:33:

> He [Solomon] spoke of trees, from the cedar that is in Lebanon to the hyssop that grows out of the wall; he spoke also of beasts, and of birds, and of reptiles, and of fish.

Two features especially elicit Alt's attention. The first of these is that the type of wisdom referred to here is a form of primitive science, or natural his-

---

[8]Cf. E. Ullendorf, *Ethiopia and the Bible* (Schweich Lectures 1967; London: 1968) 131ff.

[9]M. Noth, *I Kings 1-16, 11, 1 of BKAT* (Neukirchen-Vluyn: 1967) 223f.

[10]A. Alt, "Die Weisheit Salomos," *TLZ* 76 (1951) 139-144 ( = *Kleine Schriften* II [Munich: 1953] 90-99).

tory, which consisted of lists of different types and classes of creatures and plants. The production of lists of all kinds was one of the foremost consequences of the impact of literacy upon human intellectual development[11] and this type of wisdom is best known from the Egyptian Onomastica. It is true that the later Israelite wisdom, as found in the book of Job and to a degree also in Proverbs, makes use of an abundance of metaphors and similes drawn from the natural world.[12] The moral order is assumed in some fashion to pervade the natural order. However, this interest in birds and beasts and reptiles for their aesthetic and literary value, does not seem to be what is referred to here. Hence the second feature that Alt was concerned with is that this erudition credited to Solomon does not subsequently re-appear, either in the traditions regarding Solomon's wisdom, or in the preserved forms of Israelite wisdom. To this extent the information of 1 Kgs 4:33 possesses a kind of unexpected and random character, so that Alt suggests such forms of wisdom listing may well have been authentic to Solomon.[13]

We must, however, dismiss this argument as a rather weak and inadequate one. Clearly the author of the entire unit of 1 Kgs 4:29-34 wanted to ascribe to Solomon the fullest and most comprehensive range of wisdom accomplishments that he could. There breathes throughout the entire section a concern that the reader should be in no doubt that Solomon was a supremely wise man. It is therefore wholly in accord with such a claim that he should have included a known and widely used type of wisdom formulation in order to support his claim. The information therefore simply serves a wider purpose of the author's and cannot indicate that it was a piece of random information that he had been in possession of.

We may regard as similarly unsuccessful the attempt of R. B. Y. Scott to derive from the unexpectedness of the information contained in Prov 25:1 some clue as to the origin of Solomon's wisdom: "These also are proverbs of Solomon which the men of Hezekiah king of Judah transcribed" (or "copied," or "interpreted"; the Hebrew *hetîqû* indicates "brought forward" in some fashion). Scott argued that it was primarily the men of Hezekiah's court who composed a large number of proverbial teachings. Scott claims, however, that since Hezekiah held Solomon in high esteem, and modeled his own attempts at restoring a united Israel on Solomon's attain-

---

[11]Cf. J. Goody, "What is a List?" *The Domestication of the Savage Mind* (Cambridge: 1977) 74ff.

[12]Cf. H. Wheeler Robinson, *Inspiration and Revelation in the Old Testament,* (Oxford: 1946) 5-6.

[13]Cf. A. Alt, "Weisheit," 97.

ments, the whole notion of wisdom has been projected back upon Solomon's court.[14]

It is certainly true that the connection of "the men of Hezekiah" with proverbial sayings comes unexpectedly in Prov 25:1. It is still far from evident, however, that Hezekiah more than any other king attached a unique significance to Solomon, rather than to David the founder of the dynasty. There is moreover a far simpler explanation as to how the title in Prov 25:1 came to acquire its present form. May it not have been the case that a late scribe, faced with a collection of sayings ascribed to "the men of Hezekiah" in a book that had become linked by convention with Solomon, has simply elaborated the original heading to show that this was so? The title would then have made clear to the reader that the sayings which follow conform to what had, by his day, become the established truth that the entire book was from Solomon. Even if this argument sounds like special pleading, we must note that the information of Prov 25:1 is far too limited and uncertain as to its intention to provide a sound basis for recovering a knowledge of why Solomon came to be regarded as the author and patron of wisdom. The text appears to presuppose this tradition, rather than to have created it.

We can then consider two further avenues of investigation that have been thought by many to explain why the tradition concerning the Solomonic origin of wisdom arose in Israel. The opening verse of 1 Kings 3 provides information regarding the marriage alliance that was established between Solomon and the Pharaoh of Egypt. Even if the royal princess was only a relatively minor personage of the Pharaonic court, this concord was undoubtedly a major diplomatic *coup* for Solomon to have achieved. It must have marked a period of relative goodwill between Israel and Egypt and have been connected with other contacts of a commercial and cultural nature. Since the relationships between Israel and Egypt later turned sour (1 Kgs 11:40) and seldom thereafter were particularly happy, it has been widely assumed that the age of Solomon was an especially positive era on this front. The contacts between Israel and Egypt were stronger at this time than at any other. Since the pursuit of wisdom was particularly encouraged and advanced in Egypt, although not under the name, and since there are numerous indications of an Israelite dependance on some aspects of the Egyptian tradition, it could be argued that it was Solomon's Egyptian contact that led to the ascription of him as author of many wisdom sayings.[15] It could even be that Solomon was, or at least sought to present himself as a learned and cultured ruler after the

---

[14]R. B. Y. Scott, "Solomon and the Beginnings of Wisdom in Israel," *VTSup* 3 (1955) 262-79.

[15]Cf. E. H. Maly, *The World of David and Solomon* (Englewood Cliffs: 1966) 154; E. W. Heaton, *Solomon's New Men* (London: 1974).

style of the Pharaoh of Egypt. Undoubtedly the discovery of the certain link between much of Prov 22-23 and the Egyptian Wisdom of Amenemope opened the path to this suggestion.[16]

This view has gained popularity through G. von Rad's idea of a Solomonic "Enlightenment,"[17] and Canon E. W. Heaton's claim for the achievements of Solomon's "new men" under such Egyptian influence.[18] It is noteworthy, however, that, in spite of the claim that Solomon's wisdom surpassed that of the wise men of Egypt (1 Kgs 4:30), the Old Testament does not make anything like as much of the Egyptian associations of wisdom as one might expect. Wisdom was, in its very nature, a supremely international pursuit, and many of the most direct allusions to national wisdom traditions in the Old Testament refer to those of Arabia and Edom. There is therefore much less to tie the development of Israel's wisdom tradition uniquely to Egypt than one might suppose. This is not to deny that there were important contacts between Israelite and Egyptian teachers of wisdom, but such also existed with Edom, Arabia and almost certainly with Phoenicia also. It is questionable therefore whether "The Egyptian Connection" can have sufficed to originate the claim that Solomon was the most celebrated patron of wisdom.

Two further considerations come in for attention here. The first of these is that, in spite of the way in which biblical tradition tends to highlight the attainments of individual kings, and even to present the historical process as one of a brief highpoint, followed by a succession of low ones, before a new highpoint is reached, the realities of social and cultural history seldom conform to this. Such contacts as served to bring about a mutual exchange of wisdom sayings and the general pursuit of wisdom teaching between different national communities are likely to have been far more prolonged and continuous than to be ascribable to a single reign. They are the product of trade contacts, of the activities of prisoners taken in war, and of the many factors that led quite large communities to seek alien status in a foreign land rather than risk oppression in their own. The history of Europe is full of such constant cultural interchange, brought about through the vagaries of social and political pressures, rather than the specific aims of a particular king. The fact of Egyptian influence upon Israel's developing wisdom tradition is not to be denied, but there is little reason for supposing that it was almost wholly concentrated in the age of Solomon. Furthermore, and this point will occupy

---

[16]The earliest suggestions for a close Israelite dependance on Egyptian wisdom as evidenced from the Amen-em-ope text are to be found in H. Gressmann, *ZAW* (1924): 272-96; D. C. Simpson, *Journal of Egyptian Archaeology* 12 (1926): 232-39. Cf. also P. Humbert, *Recherches sur les sources égyptiennes de la litterature sapientale d'Israel* (Neuchatel: 1929).

[17]G. von Rad, *Old Testament Theology*, vol. 1, trans. D. Stalker (Edinburgh: 1962) 425.

[18]Cf. E. W. Heaton, *Solomon's New Men*, 28.

attention more fully in the second part of this paper, it must be argued that any suspicion that Solomon's fame for wisdom owed its origin to his contacts with Egypt would have undermined completely the purpose that the author of 1 Kgs 3, 4 and 10 wished to convey. Even if some element of fact may reside in the claim that Solomon's reputation for wisdom owed something to his links with Egypt, this fact would appear to be wholly insufficient of itself to explain its importance in the development of Israelite traditions about wisdom.

There is a further avenue of investigation which has been thought to provide a possible basis for understanding the claim to Solomon's great wisdom and his authorship of thousands of proverbial sayings. This concerns the fact that 1 Kgs 4:1-19 first lists the major officials of Solomon's administration and then the twelve officers whom he appointed over all Israel. Although the historian does not specifically claim that most of these appointments were to new offices previously unknown, or little known, in Israel, this would certainly appear to have been the case.[19] Solomon had brought about a major development of the royal palace administration, of tax collection and of the general administration of the tribal territories which things greatly weakened the power of the older tribal chiefs. Such a large-scale body of national administrators and royal servants would have required a substantial army of minor officials and public employees. It has thus become important to show that the Israelite wisdom tradition had many connections with the work and activities of such public officials. In two particular areas the activities of royal officials and of the wise men would appear to have overlapped, namely in the development of literacy for secretarial and accounting work, and for diplomatic responsibilities, which would have called for a knowledge of the languages and traditions of other nations. Thus there are certainly features of the wisdom tradition of ancient Israel which suggest that it had many close links with the royal court and that it was a form of learning particularly relevant to state administration. As the prime initiator of a much enlarged state administration it would have been quite appropriate that Solomon should have been credited with being an exemplary wise man. The claim to a Solomonic origin for wisdom could then be regarded as possessing an institutional basis in which Solomon was recognized as the ''Founder'' of an Israelite Diplomatic Corps and Civil Service.[20]

This path to understanding the claim that Solomon was a great originator of Israelite wisdom teaching could readily be combined with the recognition

---

[19]For these officials cf. R. de Vaux, *Ancient Israel*, trans. J. McHugh (London: 1961) 127-32; T. N. D. Mettinger, *Solomonic State Officials: A Study of the Civil Government Officials of the Israelite Monarchy, Coniectanea Biblica*, 5 (Lund: 1971); U. Rütersworden, *Die Beamten der israelitischen Königszeit*, BWANT 117 (Stuttgart: 1985).

[20]E. W. Heaton, *Solomon's New Men*, 47ff.

of his Egyptian contacts. Although the issue remains contested, there have been many suggestions that the Solomonic state administration was modelled on that of ancient Egypt.

This is an area of historical research where we can clearly not hope to find more than some partial items of evidence, and there is a serious danger that such partial evidence can be greatly overstressed as to its implications. We may therefore be content to draw attention to the many serious gaps which exist in such an explanation. In the first instance, it is now largely discounted that the Israelite wisdom tradition was in any way institutionalized in a body of state officials and scribes.[21] All the pointers indicate that wisdom was too widely pursued and valued for this to have been the case. Nor, in fact, are the features of Solomon's acclaimed expertise in wisdom in any very direct way linked with such administrative skills. We might regard the claim that he possessed unique insight in judicial matters as contravening this, but in fact it is the royal skill in seeing into the hidden motives of the human heart that is praised (1 Kgs 3:28). It is also very clearly evident that the kind of wisdom attainment that is acclaimed for Solomon in 1 Kgs 4:29-34, and then later in the books of Proverbs and Ecclesiastes, had nothing to do with his responsibility for having set up an elaborate governmental administrative body. Indeed one may be certain that the latter would not have fitted very well into the overall regard for Solomon's wisdom that the author of 1 Kings wanted to create.

We may summarize the overall conclusion we are led to in this short review of scholars' endeavors to understand the origin of the tradition regarding Solomon's wisdom. Since the scholar's views are not altogether mutually exclusive of each other, it is possible to claim that, even though no one view in itself is sufficient to explain the origin of such a tradition, taken together, two, or perhaps even three of them, do carry some weight. The cumulative effect would be important for the historian to consider, but, even so, we would be well advised to proceed with caution before concluding that we possess clear explanation for the rise of the tradition concerning Solomon's great wisdom.

I should like to suggest that there is another line of approach which can provide us with a far more helpful and usable basis for understanding the rise of this tradition. This approach does not deny that some of the features we have examined may have contributed something to the overall picture but it would indicate that the major impetus for the rise of this tradition lies in an altogether different direction.

---

[21]Cf. R. N. Whybray, *The Intellectual Trdition in the Old Testament*, BZAW 135 (Berlin, New York: 1974). F. W. Golka, "Die Israelitische Weisheitsschule oder 'Des Kaisers neue Kleider,' " *VT* 33 (1983) 257-70.

Several years ago in an essay on the cluster of traditions concerning the origins of kingship with Saul (1 Kgs 8-12) I suggested that it is odd that Saul should have been accused, at least by inference, of a style of oppressive and tyrannical kingship which most appropriately belongs to Solomon (1 Sam 8:11-18).[22] The "ways" of the king of which Samuel forewarns the people fit the reputation of Solomon very precisely and evidently provide the substance of the demands put to Rehoboam that he should lessen the royal burdens imposed by his father (1 Kgs 12:4). His refusal to accede to these demands brought about the division of the kingdom, with all its further consequences (1 Kgs 12:16-20). There is accordingly a startling inconsistency in the manner in which the Deuteronomistic Historian goes about his explanation of the causes of the disruption after Solomon's death. He provides all the essential factual information to show clearly the oppressive aspects of Solomon's reign which were the real cause. Yet he carefully avoids stating that this was the reason for the break-up of the Kingdom of David and instead offers a rather contrived "religious" explanation associated with the high-places of foreign gods (1 Kgs 11:1-13). The reason why he has proceeded in this way is not hard to find. It is not his obsessive preoccupation with the dangers of tolerating the shrines of non-Yahwistic deities, nor his sensitivity to the seductive wiles of foreign women. The reason is, in spite of everything, he is concerned to assure the reader that God himself held fast to his promise to the dynasty of David concerning its right to fill the throne of Israel in perpetuity (1 Kgs 11:13; see 2 Sam 7:16).[23] Solomon may have been an oppressive tyrant, but he was a Davidic tyrant who therefore needed to be tolerated.

We can also usefully note that the tensions created for the Deuteronomistic School by the excesses of Solomon are made evident in the law of the king set forth in Deut 17:14-20. Quite directly, the list of what the king must not do in Deut 17:16-17 is modelled on the experience of Solomon, whereas the emphasis upon "him whom Yahweh your God will choose" (v 15) points to a dynastic commitment of some kind. It must surely reflect the tradition of the divine promise to the dynasty of David in 2 Sam 7:1-16.

When we give all of these considerations their due weight we can see why the Deuteronomistic Historian who has composed the account of Solomon's reign in 1 Kings 1-11 placed considerable emphasis upon the claim that Solomon was a supremely wise ruler. It is essentially the Deuteronomist's own

---

[22]R. E. Clements, "The Deuteronomistic Interpretation of the Founding of the Monarchy in I Sam. viii," *VT* 24 (1974) 398-410.

[23]For the importance of the divine covenant with the dynasty of David for an understanding of the political theology of the Deuteronomistic History, cf. D. J. McCarthy "II Samuel 7 and the Structure of the Deuteronomic History," *JBL* 84 (1965) 131-38 ( = *Institution and Narrative: Collected Essays,* Analecta Biblica 108 (Rome: 1985) 127-34).

claim that this was so. Undoubtedly there must have been some already existing factors which have led to a presentation along these lines. Foremost among these we should place the fact that there existed, certainly in Israel and almost as certainly in the traditions of wisdom of other nations, a claim that kings were supremely wise persons:

> Inspired judgments are on the lips of a king;
>        his mouth does not err in judgment. (Prov 16:10)

A tradition concerning "royal wisdom" finds some representation in the Old Testament, a tradition which must once have been very much larger in its scope.[24] According to it, the king is endowed with wisdom as a divine gift, while others must seek it by careful training and observation. The stories of Solomon's dream vision in which he asks for this gift of wisdom, and of the judgment concerning the child claimed by the two harlots, both belong wholly to such a tradition. They are both stories that could have been told of any king, once the claim to a special kind of royal wisdom was conceded. In fact they may well have been told of other rulers besides Solomon, although this is something that we cannot know. What is evident is that a well attested tradition concerning royal wisdom has been given a specific focus in the case of Solomon.

Since we have other indications that the Deuteronomist had fundamental political motives for wanting to create as good an image of Solomon as possible, then it is open to suggest that he himself has been responsible for this, although it could well be the case that some predecessor had already done so. Nevertheless, the basic contention would stand that Solomon has been uniquely credited with being an exponent of wisdom, because his reputation stood in the greatest need of it. The deeply rooted, amply justified and long remembered tradition concerning Solomon's oppressive rule over Israel, which received some later emulation in the activities of Jehoiakim (B.C. 609-598; see Jer 22:13-19), had led to a complete rejection by many in Israel of the claims of the Davidic dynasty. It is noteworthy that the commitment to the dynasty of David is made the central point at issue in the rebellion against Jeroboam (1 Kgs 12:16). There are therefore good reasons for accepting the view that it was precisely the question of the claims of the dynasty of David which remained the major point of division between Judah and Israel until the

---

[24]For such a tradition of "royal wisdom" cf. N. W. Porteous "Royal Wisdom," *VTSup* 3 (1955) 247-61 ( = *Living the Mystery, Collected Essays* [Oxford: 1967] 77-92). Evidence of such a tradition concerning royal wisdom is to be found in various proverbial sayings (e.g. Prov 14:28,35; 16:10,12,14,15; 19:10,12; 20:2,8,18,26,28). Whether such a tradition of royal wisdom represents a feature of folk tradition (as F. W. Golka, "Die Israelitische Weisheitschule" suggests), or whether it points to a close link between wisdom circles and the royal court (as N. W. Porteous), may be left aside in the present context.

eventual collapse of the Northern Kingdom under Assyrian domination. The Deuteronomist therefore has been conscientious enough to recognize the justice of most of the grievances nursed in the Northern Kingdom against the rule of Solomon, but politically loyal enough to insist that God had nevertheless held fast to his promise to the house of David. It is in pursuing this difficult line of compromise that he has focused upon Solomon a number of traditional assertions regarding royal wisdom. A form of apologetic which had originally been part of a widespread attempt to popularize the institution of monarchy in general among wisdom teachers, has been turned into a defence of the claims of the Davidic dynasty.

The above would seem to be by far the most plausible explanation for the presentation of the stories regarding Solomon's wisdom in 1 Kgs 3 and 4:29-34. Possibly there were already some extant elements in the court traditions of Jerusalem concerning Solomon's great wisdom which made it easy for the Deuteronomist to expand them in this fashion. If so, then they have simply provided him with useful supporting ideas. Far more central than any of them is the evident desire that the Deuteronomist has shown to present as acceptable a picture of Solomon as was possible under the circumstances. Nor has he pursued this line out of any special interest in Solomon's personal reputation or of any particular feature of wisdom. It has been done out of a concern to elicit support for the Davidic dynasty in his own day. If Israel is to have kings, then they must be kings of the line of David.

One may question whether such an explanation is equally as valid for the tradition of 1 Kgs 10:1-13 concerning the visit of the Queen of Sheba as it is for that of the traditions of 1 Kgs 3-4. It may be suggested, however, that here another aspect of the wisdom tradition has been exploited in order to serve the author's purpose. This concerns the traditional connection between wisdom and prosperity. If the basis of the story concerning the Queen of Sheba's visit lies in the trade links between Israel and Africa, then these links have offered an opportunity to draw attention to the connection between wisdom and wealth. So far as we can tell the caravan trade between Phoenicia, Africa and Mesopotamia went on in a more or less unbroken sequence for two, or three, millennia. Solomon's contribution to it (1 Kgs 5:1; 9:26-28; 10:14-15, 22, 26-29) must therefore have consisted primarily in a desire to gain advantage of it, rather than to have initiated it in any new way. In this too, therefore, the Deuteronomist would appear to have been responsible for using the tradition regarding Solomon's trading links as an opportunity for further enhancement of his reputation for wisdom. Further, by insisting upon the great wealth entering Israel at this time, he sought to alleviate the bitterness caused by Solomon's exactions. He is suggesting that, although the people paid exorbitant taxes, they could afford it!

We have to admit that we know very little regarding the economic conditions that prevailed in Israel throughout the Old Testament period. The indications are that Solomon greatly impoverished his territory (1 Kgs 9:10-14; see Deut 17:16). By this means intense bitterness arose against the monarchy in general as an institution, and the house of David in particular. It is this bitterness that is reflected in Samuel's recitation of the ways of the king in 1 Sam 8:11-18. The tradition of Solomon's wisdom therefore has been exploited in another direction in order to provide a further attempt at softening the reputation of a ruler who had done so much harm to the Davidic dynasty and its acceptability to Israel.

We may bring this examination to a conclusion therefore by summarizing what we can learn from 1 Kgs 1-11 regarding the origin of the tradition concerning Solomon's great wisdom. As it now stands the material forms the central basis for the author's contention that God had blessed Israel under the reign of Solomon. The reason why he has gone to such lengths to do this is to be found in the political commitment to the Davidic dynasty which he, the Deuteronomist author, still regarded as valid for his own day. The elements which have provided the basis for the claim concerning Solomon's unique skill as an exponent of wisdom are twofold: the tradition of a unique form of royal wisdom offered a basis for the claim that Solomon excelled in this gift. Secondly, the tradition that wisdom leads to the acquisition of wealth offered a platform for explaining the ambitious and excessive building works which Solomon undertook and the heavy taxation which he imposed. It could indeed be the case that there was available some other item of information available to the Deuteronomistic author of 1 Kings, or even several such items, which meant that some popular recognition of Solomon as a wise king was already widely known. If this was the case, it is not really clear from 1 Kings what this information was, and it can hardly have been felt to be very important for the author's purposes. In order to defend the Davidic dynasty the Deuteronomistic author needed all the support he could find in order to make the figure of Solomon acceptable to a kingdom which had found in it a reason for abandoning the Davidic dynasty. He found such support in some fundamental characteristics of the wisdom tradition itself.

# ZELOPHEHAD'S DAUGHTERS

KATHARINE DOOB SAKENFELD
PRINCETON THEOLOGICAL SEMINARY
PRINCETON NJ 08542

The story of the daughters of Zelophehad (Num 27 and 36) has received surprisingly little attention in recent literature. The few references available deal primarily with the value of the text for our knowledge of how law was created and codified in Israel and in the ancient Near East more generally. The purpose of the present essay is to identify a series of problems that may underlie the inattention to these chapters, to indicate something of the inter-locking of the problems, and to make some tentative probes toward solution of some of these.

Num 27:1-11 relates in a straightforward and even entertaining way how the five daughters of Zelophehad approach Moses to request that since their father had died "for his own sin" and without leaving any sons, they should be allowed to take possession of his inheritance in the promised land. Moses consults the deity and the women receive a favorable reply. A generalized law concerning the order of inheritance is announced by Moses in connection with the specific decision. After considerable intervening material, the issue recurs abruptly in the concluding chapter of Numbers. The male relatives of Zelophehad are unhappy with the possibility that marriage of his daughters may lead to land being transferred out of their own tribe. In response, God's decree through Moses is that these women must marry within their own tribe, so that inheritance will not be transferred from one tribe to another. Again, a more generalized law follows, although it is not cast in classic casuistic format. The text is rounded off by the narrator's "they lived happily ever after":

the daughters marry according to Moses' ruling, and their inheritance remains within their tribe. A brief paragraph in Josh 17:3-6 reports that the command of Moses was carried out.[1]

The first problem to be considered is the separation between the two parts of the Numbers narrative. It is commonly noted that the book of Numbers is among the most disjointed of the entire Hebrew canon. Indeed, there is little agreement among commentators as to the general outline of the book.[2] Of the various major divisions proposed for the book, a break at chapter 26 seems most probable to me.[3] It is at least clear that in the received form of the text chapter 27 is tied closely to 26 by anticipatory notices appearing in 26:33 and 26:52-56. Here Zelophehad's special situation (no sons) is made explicit and the rule of inheritance according to the "names" of the ancestral tribes is stated. Verses 54 and 56 seem quite appropriate to their context immediately following the enumeration of the adult male population of each tribe, but their emphasis on allotment proportional to tribal size can also be read as anticipatory of the concern expressed by Zelophehad's male relatives in chapter 36. Why are the two chapters so far apart?

From a purely narrative standpoint, the delay until after the conquest and apportionment of Transjordan heightens the reader's retrospective surprise that the relatives had accepted the chapter 27 ruling uncontested. We are not told whether they had been brooding over the matter all during the intervening events, or whether the long-range implications of Moses' pronouncement suddenly dawned upon them.[4] The delay also allows the question of land for future generations to become the climax of the tetrateuch; while the people are poised to cross the Jordan, land distribution becomes the immediate backdrop for Deuteronomy's exhortations to faithfulness so that future generations may continue to live in the land.

And yet such literary observations fall short of addressing the redactional puzzle of the conclusion of Numbers. To approach this puzzle, however ten-

---

[1]The verbal and structural parallels of Josh 17:3-4 and Num 27 suggests literary dependence. It is possible that a historical fragment concerning the Manassites underlies the tradition, but it is no longer recoverable.

[2]See D. T. Olson, *The Death of the Old and the Birth of the New: The Framework of the Book of Numbers and the Pentateuch* (Chico: Scholars, 1985) for a comprehensive survey of the various outlines proposed over the last century.

[3]Olson, *Death*, interprets the theology of the book as a whole in terms of its two-generation structure, observing a pattern of disobedience (chaps. 1-25) followed by obedience (chaps. 26-36). M. Noth, pursuing a redactional rather than a literary question, attributed all of chaps. 26-36 (except 27:12-23) to various late redactors (*A History of Pentateuchal Traditions*, [Englewood Cliffs: Prentice-Hall, 1972] 9, 18-19).

[4]Likewise, we are not told of the background of the daughters' approach to Moses. This is typical of the widely recognized reticence of Hebrew narrative concerning the thoughts of its characters and other background features.

tatively, one must consider whether the present shape of Numbers was fin-
alized before or after Deuteronomy came to be viewed as part of the
foundational (Torah) story of Israel. This difficult question can hardly be
considered in detail here, but the purpose of the two parts of the Zelophehad
narrative ought not to be addressed in isolation from it.

With the majority of commentators I would view chapter 36 as an addition to be attributed to a hand later than that responsible for chapter 27, both
because chapter 36 seems intended to close a loophole in the earlier legislation and because of its distance from that chapter. Differences in detail and
vocabulary, conveniently detailed in G. B. Gray's 1903 ICC commentary,[5]
are thus accounted for. The assignment of the chapters to possible authors
such as P, P[SUP], R[P], or independent supplementers is much disputed, depending on the scholars' views of P as an independent narrator or as a nar-
rator-redactor and their views of P as concerned for cult only or for land as
well. A number of scholars (Noth, Smend, Rendtorff, Auld) have noted the
affinities of much of Numbers 26-36 with material in the Deuteronomistic
History and have argued that most or all of this material was inserted after
DtH came to be regarded as a continuation of the tetrateuchal narrative.[6] I
believe this view is correct with regard to much of this material; I am, however, inclined to attribute Numbers 26-27 to an initial priestly narrator-re-
dactor of the tetrateuch.

Given the extremely miscellaneous character of the last nine chapters of
Numbers, it is difficult to know why the supplementer would not have inserted the material of chapter 36 immediately after 27:11. Accepting chapters
26-27 as the original ''conclusion'' to the tetrateuch (excepting of course the
death of Moses now reported at the end of Deuteronomy) makes the odd location of chapter 36 somewhat more understandable. Unless one is prepared
to argue that the materials have been deliberately split apart, it is simplest to
presume that chapter 36 was added as a final appendix after the book of Numbers was complete as an individual scroll. Thus the attribution of chapter 36
to a very late hand, post-Ezra, and the recognition of a Pentateuchal unit,
seems most probable.

What then of the purpose of each of the chapters concerning Zelophehad's daughters? Despite the obvious literary connections of the two texts,
and the plain intent of the second to close a loophole in the first, I wish to
suggest that the two chapters are in fact focusing upon two different (even
though not totally unrelated) questions, each of which has its own importance

---

[5]*Numbers* (Edinburgh: T. & T. Clark) 477.

[6]Olson (*Death*, 50-53) provides a convenient summary of the differences between the major proponents of this approach.

in a patriarchal society. These are, on the one hand, the question of preservation of the father's name (chap. 27) and, on the other, the question of property rights (chap. 36).

The story of chapter 27 is one that readily invites our participation through the act of imagination. For both women and men it is important to learn by entering imaginatively into the lives of the characters, even as people have done for generations with more familiar stories such as the near-sacrifice of Isaac.[7] Numbers 27 presents a narrative in which those with the least power and the most to lose dare to challenge the epitome of authority, God's own spokesperson Moses, and even implicitly to suggest that God's own decrees may have overlooked an important point.[8] The daughters' challenge, moreover, is given not in private but in the most public arena possible--at the entrance of the tent of meeting, before Moses, Eleazer, the officials, and the whole congregation. The text is silent about the reaction of all the audience except Moses, but one may imagine the responses of the onlookers (shock, amazement, incredulity) and play with the adjectives they may have whispered to one another concerning these women--foolhardy, daring, assertive (aggressive), uppity. . . . Did someone perhaps whisper more softly "justified," even before Moses' response?[9] The text is equally silent concerning the women's own feelings as they came to stand before Moses. Were they frightened or self-confident, clear or tentative about their decision to speak, of one mind or divided about how to proceed? Who among the five urged the others on? Who dragged her feet and accompanied the others only reluc-

---

[7]For the importance of this activity, see especially Elisabeth Schüssler Fiorenza's discussion of "a feminist hermeneutics of creative actualization [that] allows women to enter the biblical story with the help of historical imagination, artistic recreation, and liturgical ritualization." *Bread Not Stone: The Challenge of Feminist Biblical Interpretation* (Boston: Beacon, 1984) 20.

[8]It is this implicit questioning of divine decree, together with the generalizing legislative result, that makes this example stand out even among other biblical narratives of the weak appealing to the powerful for justice.

[9]Several scholars have focused on the Zelophehad material as illustration of how case law came into being in ancient Near Eastern (or at least biblical) culture. See J. Weingreen, "The Case of the Daughters of Zelophchad" [sic], *VT* 16 (1966): 518-22, and R. Westbrook, "Biblical and Cuneiform Law Codes," *RB* 92 (1985): 247-64. Westbrook's four stages (decision in a case without precedent, anonymous rule, casuistic formulation, and compilation of list with logical variations) are helpful in elucidating a general process. What is glossed over is the question of how a case would come before the authorities for decision. In Num 15:32-35 the people bring the case by challenging the action of a man who turns out to have defiled the Sabbath. In Num 9 certain men denied the privilege of the Passover bring the problem of their ritual uncleanness to Moses. Only the Zelophehad story considers a non-ritual matter, and there are no further significant biblical or extra-biblical parallels. It seems unlikely that women would have had frequent occasion to appeal to village, regional, or national authorities in precedent-setting cases.

tantly? How did each feel as Moses announced Yahweh's favorable response? The scene is compelling and thought-provoking.

And yet it is not for the purpose of these imaginative questions that the writer preserved the story for us, or that it came into the canon. The story is told to deal with a man's problem in a patriarchal culture, namely, the tragedy of a man dead without male issue--and to legislate mitigation of such tragedy for all Israel. The daughters' statement of their case could be interpreted at the literary level as a clever ploy to get what they really wanted, the land inheritance. After all, the male authorities of the community would be more likely to be persuaded by the need to preserve Zelophehad's name than by any appeal to his daughters' "rights." Nonetheless, the text as a reflector of cultural values probably places on the surface what most men and women of the culture were concerned about, the male family line. The boundary between literary and cultural-contextual reading is not always easy to determine; but in this case attending to both sides of the boundary enables the reader to perceive both patriarchy and freeing from patriarchy in a single text.

Israel's understanding of the relationship between continuation of the father's name and the "possession" of an "inheritance" is difficult to delineate with precision. The implication seems to be that the name is preserved by descendants' being in possession of ancestral property. The custom of levirate marriage is the better known means of accomplishing the preservation of a man's name (see Deut 25:5-10); and it has been argued that the tradition of Numbers 27 cannot be familiar with the levirate custom. But this scarcely seems a necessary conclusion, for in the case of Zelophehad in its narrative setting, one must assume that his wife also has died along with the first generation of Israel in the wilderness. Nor are his own brothers presumed to be living. The question can only be how to preserve his name among the second generation when his own generation is totally lacking. Davies has suggested that the purpose of the levirate marriage was not only to preserve the dead husband's name, but also secondarily could be "to prevent alienation of the ancestral estate."[10] By focusing on the "secondary" matter of ancestral estate, Numbers 27 addresses the question of how the name can be preserved when the levir cannot be invoked. The land inheritance now becomes primary, with the remembering of the father's name dependent upon it.

----

[10]E. W. Davies, "Inheritance Rights and the Hebrew Levirate Marriage: Part 1," *VT* 31 (1981) 138-44. The clearest text offering direct support for Davies' interpretation is Ruth 4:10, where name and inheritance are mentioned together. His agreement with Noth that Num 27 presumes preservation of a name is possible *only* in conjunction with inherited property (141) is not warranted, in my view, since the alternate possibility of preservation through levirate marriage is precluded by the narrative context. Thus the Numbers text ought not to be used directly in support of the dual function of levirate marriage.

In this regard, Snaith's observation that the text focuses on allocation of land has some merit,[11] although the way in which he has argued the point needs modification. Granting his emphasis that the preservation of Zelophehad's name is associated with land allocation because of the narrative structure, the more general issue of the ordering of inheritance is still present in the text (in the form of the casuistic legislation) and must be accounted for. To explain the presence of both themes, one may posit that an old fragment of remembered tradition about Zelophehad's daughters is used to illustrate the author's concern for proper apportionment of the new land, and general inheritance custom is easily incorporated into this agenda. The focal question of the preservation of Zelophehad's name provides the connecting link between these two themes.

Moses' pronouncement of legislation concerning inheritance (vv 8-11) may be heard in various ways. A literary reading may rejoice that daughters were now given priority over other, male relatives. It may rejoice that the ruling for Zelophehad's daughters was not a one-time exception but was generalized to provide opportunity for other such women. A more cultural-contextual approach may focus instead on the patriarchal reality that daughters could inherit only in the absence of any male offspring. The priority of daughters over other male relatives in casuistic inheritance law is known from at least one legal fragment from elsewhere in the Ancient Near East. The text in question may be a part of Lipit-Ishtar's laws (early second millennium) but even this is not certain,[12] and we are reminded of the dangers of simplistic comparisons of the status of women in various parts of the ancient world. Our evidence does not permit any broad generalization even of the supposed custom, much less of the extent to which it was actually applied. And of course the ruling would be of significance only to those families who actually could lay claim to some property.

Whether one emphasizes the freeing or the limiting aspects of the legislation, its corollary is made clear in chapter 36: in post-exilic Israel (and possibly much earlier if the legislation reflects older custom), it was important in Israel to control the transfer of property by restricting the marriage options of certain women who did hold property.[13] Chapter 36 picks up on the nar-

---

[11]N. H. Snaith, "The Daughters of Zelophehad," *VT* 16 (1966) 124-27. Snaith's claim to explain all of the text as aetiology for Cisjordan Manasseh seems strained.

[12]See M. Civil, "New Sumerian Law Fragments," in *Studies in Honor of Benno Landsberger on His Seventy-fifth Birthday, University of Chicago Oriental Institute Assyriological Studies* 16 (1965) 4-6.

[13]A modern expression such as holding property "in their own right" is probably not appropriate here. At least in the case of Zelophehad's daughters, the land would seem to be held in behalf of the deceased father. The restriction of marriage emphasizes that no woman who

rative theme and structure of chapter 27, although its content focuses primarily on the inheritance legislation; the matter of the father's name seems no longer of interest. The male heads of ancestral houses of the Gileadite clan to which Zelophehad belonged suggest that the daughters' future marriages may cause his land to be lost to other tribes. Moses, again at God's instruction, announces that marriages of the daughters must be to men within the "clan of the tribe of their father." The stated purpose of the legislation, both for the specific case (v 7) and for the generalized rule (v 9), is tied to maintaining *tribal* holdings intact; but the legislation itself is much narrower, with its restriction to the individual *clan*.[14]

From a literary perspective one notes especially the silence, indeed the non-presence, of the five daughters of Zelophehad in the scene before Moses. Only the leaders and the heads of the ancestral houses hear the complaint of the male relatives. The daughters appear narratively only in the concluding vv 10-11 reporting their obedient marriages. It is true that the male relatives are not specified as present in chapter 27 when the daughters make their petition, but they are included implicitly among "all the congregation," whereas there is no textual ground for supposing the presence of the women in chapter 36.[15]

Culturally it is certain that possession of arable land would make any woman in Israel extremely desirable as a marriage prospect. The male relatives see themselves potentially disadvantaged economically by Moses' earlier decision and now seek a way to circumscribe those possible losses by maintaining clan control of the land in question. In this case they only present the problem; Moses presents the solution of controlling the marriage options of the daughters.

We do not have any definitive evidence as to how marriage partners in Israel were generally selected. Biblical narratives provide examples of both

---

"possesses an inheritance" can do what she pleases with property, so that it is not hers "in her own right" in the popular modern sense of the phrase. Neither of the two other narrative texts alluding to women's possession of land (Ruth 4:3 and 2 Kgs 8:5-6) makes clear how the woman came to hold the property mentioned.

[14]The ending of 36:8 in fact provides the basic clue as to the cultural purpose of such legislation, with its general allusion to possessing an "ancestral inheritance" ("the inheritance of his fathers"), a phrase which can be read very generally to focus on male property rights. The broadening to a tribal level introduces theological overtones related to the religious understanding of Israel's structure in ancient times and in the idealized future. For a socio-economic interpretation of the "clan" (Heb. מִשְׁפָּחָה, rendered "family" in some translations) level of kinship structure, see N. Gottwald, *The Tribes of Yahweh* (Maryknoll: Orbis, 1979) 257-70.

[15]As indicated earlier in this essay, a variety of differences in detail bespeaks a different hand from that responsible for chap. 27, despite the general similarity in outline. Note especially the "whole congregation" and "tent of meeting," only in chap. 27, and the "heads of ancestral houses," only in chap. 36. The daughters' names also appear in different order.

the man's family and the man himself taking initiative to secure the desired woman, but there are no instances recorded of women themselves selecting a marriage partner.[16] If we assume the options suggested by the biblical examples, then the legislation of Numbers 36 would have functioned to reduce competition among males by eliminating from the scene most of the potential suitors for Zelophehad's daughters. Individuals or families from other clans seeking to expand their land holdings could not acquire new property by this means. Inheritance would remain within the clan of the tribe. And it is this correct disposition of the inheritance, not any "rights" of the daughters or even the father's name, that is of real interest to the narrator of Numbers 36.

Three problems remain to be highlighted concerning this marriage law for the daughters of Zelophehad: to whom could they in fact be married, why would post-exilic Israel have been concerned about the problem the narrative addresses, and what is the function of the reference to jubilee in 36:4.

First, the biblical tradition is clear that marriage within the Israelite community is the norm, and exceptions are treated as such. The question of what proximity of relationship was "too close," that is, incestuous, has been more difficult to understand. An important step forward in our understanding of the marriage rules of Leviticus 18 and 20 appears in the work of Susan Rattray.[17] She has unraveled the technical terms in these texts in such a way as to show that marriage to a father's brother's daughter (the practical outcome of the Zelophehad case, 36:10) was regularly permitted. The Zelophehad case ruling thus does not, contrary to some commentators, introduce permission for a closer-than-normal marriage relationship; it only prohibits too-distant possibilities.[18] Whether the too-distant point is bounded by the tribe or by the clan is not stated consistently by the text, as noted above. It seems probable (again in contrast to the view prevalent in commentaries) that the clan limitation is the primary focus, since the preservation of tribal territories would be an automatic consequence of intra-clan marriage.

Second, this focus on the clan helps in understanding how this material could have immediate socio-economic application to a post-exilic community in which tribal structure was not a prominent feature of social organi-

---

[16]The initiatives of Ruth and Tamar with regard to levirate obligations ought not to be considered in this category.

[17]"Marriage Rules, Kinship Terms and Family Structure in the Bible," *Society of Biblical Literature 1987 Seminar Papers*, ed. K. H. Richards (Atlanta: Scholars, 1987) 537-44.

[18]The possibility of regularized tribal exogamy, claimed by some on the basis of the story of the Benjaminites in Judges 21, seems to me unwarranted, since the evidence is limited to this one text. The fact that some tribes swore not to give their women in marriage to another shows only that marriage outside the tribe was permitted, not that marriage within the tribe was prohibited.

zation. The story with its land transfer restrictions is preserved not solely in relation to some idealized time of restoration of the twelve-tribe community, but as a practical guideline for inheritance in the post-exilic situation. Patrimonial rights are thus guarded even in the context of ancient tradition allowing for daughters' inheritance. While it is not impossible that the limitation on marriage for such daughters likewise goes back to very ancient tradition in Israel and/or in other parts of the Near East, the point here is simply that this law could be of considerable importance to the community even in the absence of an active tribal structure.

Finally, there remains the problem of the argument about the jubilee presented by Zelophehad's male relatives: "And when the jubilee of the people of Israel comes, then their inheritance will be added to the inheritance of the tribe to which they belong; and their inheritance will be taken away from the inheritance of the tribe of our fathers" (36:4). It is widely agreed that the story assumes that any "inheritance" held by a daughter when there was no son will become part of her husband's property when she marries.[19] Otherwise, the ruling could not accomplish its purpose. Why then the point about jubilee? Noth[20] and Snaith[21] have argued that this reference to the jubilee is inappropriate both literarily and factually. Noth suggests that the allusion is literarily inappropriate because it assumes no change at the jubilee, rather than reversion to original owners, while Snaith objects that the jubilee law in Leviticus 25 applies only to land sold, not to land inherited, and thus is not applicable here.

Against their analyses, I would suggest that the reference to jubilee does form an appropriate climax to the relatives' complaint, and that it should not be presumed to be in contradiction to the jubilee tradition of Leviticus 25. The structure of Num 36:4 closely parallels that of v 3, to be sure. But this can be understood as emphatic, rather than as redundant. *Even* in the time of jubilee, the change of property ownership made by the daughters' marriages will stand. Precisely because there will be no change it is necessary to limit their marriages. Similarly, it is true that their possession is an inheritance, *not* sold to them; but precisely for this reason it does *not* come under the jubilee

---

[19]Note that the text is referring only to the daughter's "inheritance" (Heb. נַחֲלָה), not to any other real or material property associated with marriage. R. Westbrook's massive study, "Old Babylonian Marriage Law" (unpublished dissertation, Yale University, 1982), reveals the remarkable complexity of legal issues surrounding marriage in one culture of the Ancient Near East. Vol. II, ch. 5 (257-314) deals with property rights. No analogies to the Zelophehad case arise, but the variety of contingencies considered in the Old Babylonian setting serves as warning against any incautious generalizing from the very scanty biblical data.

[20]M. Noth, *Numbers: A Commentary* (OTL; Philadelphia: Westminster, 1968) 257.

[21]"The Daughters of Zelophehad," 127.

ruling and would *not* be returned to Zelophehad's line. Additional legislation is therefore needed to safeguard the intent of the jubilee. Both Noth and Snaith have made correct observations, but the implications of each observation point to the appropriateness of the jubilee reference as a climactic argument, rather than to its intrusiveness.

Thus the climax of the appeal by the male relatives of Zelophehad brings the story full circle. The daughters' initial concern, explicated in terms of preserving the father's name, was narratively inseparable from the problem of allocation of land. Now the concern of the heads of Gildead's fathers' houses keeps the issue of land allocation in the foreground by raising the question of its perpetual validity. If even the jubilee cannot eliminate the possibility of permanent transfer outside the tribe,[22] then surely Moses must act. And indeed, the ideal of perpetual allocation is affirmed by Moses' pronouncement that the land shall not be transferred from tribe to tribe.

To recapitulate, we have seen that while the story of the daughters of Zelophehad may refract ancient fragments of tradition concerning the settlement of Cisjordan, these are no longer the center of the narrator's purpose in chapter 27. Rather, the focus of chapter 27 is on the preservation of the father's name by the proper distribution of his inheritance, with the issue of land allocation as the narrative context for establishing the more general principle. While the story functions literarily to portray those of least power bringing a challenge to the holder of greatest power, this reality is ancillary to the narrator's purpose in preserving the story.

This relative insignificance of the women themselves is underscored by their non-appearance in the supplemental story of another presentation to Moses recorded in chapter 36. Here the supplementer's concern has moved away from family name to concentrate on the economic matter of family property. The male relatives' very practical concern for economic control is given a double religious grounding--the original principle of equitable allocation among the tribes, and the "for all time" jubilee principle of the preservation of that allocation. The author of chapter 36 not only closes a loophole in the inheritance legislation; he also closes a loophole in the jubilee legislation in the same stroke. Thus like Numbers 27, Numbers 36 has a dual function. It provides for a specific practical legislative problem in Israel (marriage restrictions on women holding property inherited from their fathers), while at the same time dealing with the religious issue of land allocation. Chapter

---

[22]Most scholars do not believe that the jubilee was observed as a regular practice in Israel, and possibly not even once. It is generally regarded as an ideal expressive of Israel's ethical vision of life in community under God's sovereignty. For a convenient summary see chap. 2 of S. H. Ringe's *Jesus, Liberation, and the Biblical Jubilee* (Philadelphia: Fortress, 1985).

27 opens the discussion by dealing with original land allocation; chapter 36 closes the matter by dealing with land allocation for the idealized future.

What then of the daughters? What of Mahlah, Noah, Hoglah, Milcah, and Tirzah? Despite the narrator's larger intent, and despite the impossibility of ascertaining from the Joshua narrative what land may have been assigned to them, at least the tradition saw fit to remember their names. Perhaps we too, so many generations later, should seek to learn their names, as symbols of those who challenged power, achieved a measure of justice, and learned something of what those engaged in struggle experience all too often: "two steps forward, one step back," with those in authority counting the step back as a step ahead.

# RELIGIOUS CONVERSION AND THE SOCIETAL ORIGINS OF ANCIENT ISRAEL

NORMAN K. GOTTWALD
NEW YORK THEOLOGICAL SEMINARY
NEW YORK NY 10001

On the basis of a textual exegesis of how non-Israelites could become Israelites in biblical times, Jacob Milgrom has called into doubt the hypothesis that Israel originated by means of a social revolution chiefly of native Canaanites,[1] as advanced in variant forms by George E. Mendenhall and Norman K. Gottwald.[2] By focusing on what he takes to be a "tacit assumption" of the revolutionary model, namely, a presupposition that the phenomenon of religious conversion was operative in earliest Israel, Milgrom concludes that "religious conversion is neither attested nor possible in ancient Israel before the second temple period."[3]

In pursuing his argument, Milgrom distinguishes two ways of becoming an Israelite other than by birth: 1) one way was an immediate affiliation to the religion through conversion which at the same time conferred full member-

---

[1]J. Milgrom, "Religious Conversion and the Revolt Model for the Formation of Israel," *JBL* 101 (1982): 169-76.

[2]G. E. Mendenhall, "The Hebrew Conquest of Palestine," *BA* 25 (1962): 66-87 = *BAR* 3 (1970): 100-20, and *The Tenth Generation: The Origins of the Biblical Tradition* (Baltimore: Johns Hopkins, 1973); N. K. Gottwald, *The Tribes of Yahweh: A Sociology of the Religion of Liberated Israel, 1250-1050 B.C.E.* (Maryknoll: Orbis, 1979; 2nd corrected printing, 1981), and "Two Models for the Origin of Ancient Israel: Social Revolution or Frontier Development," *The Quest for the Kingdom of God. Studies in Honor of George E. Mendenhall*, ed. H. B. Huffmon et al. (Winona Lake: Eisenbrauns, 1983) 5-24.

[3]Milgrom, 169.

ship in Israel; 2) a second route was to marry an Israelite and, after some generations, one's descendants would assimilate into full standing in Israel. In substance, Milgrom contends that one could "convert" to Israel only after the exile, whereas before that one had to "assimilate" slowly through intermarriage.

To fill out a conceptual apparatus for thinking about the subject of conversion and its pertinence for Israelite origins, I want to propose two further understandings of how people might join Israel; 3) a third mode was absorption through territorial conquest resulting in voluntary or compulsory observance of the religion, a mode probably most extensively practiced in the Davidic conquests of previously Canaanite regions adjacent to Israelite tribal holdings; and 4) a fourth pathway was to have lived among the various peoples who joined together in the highlands of Canaan to form the people Israel and to worship the God Yahweh. We can call this primal mode of becoming Israelite "participation in the originative formation of Israel."

Milgrom skirts the mode of absorption by conquest when he dismisses the ḥērem as a piece of historical fiction but does not propose what happened to all those Canaanites who were not destroyed by Israel, other than to allow that many of them, especially in northern Israel, may have assimilated through intermarriage. As for the process by which Israel came into being, Milgrom does not entertain the slightest consideration of the possibility that the "charter members" of earliest Israel, either in sizable numbers or in toto, consisted of people who had previously known other identities and who were now "changing" (converting?) to a new identity.

In this response to Milgrom, I shall argue that he is mistaken to believe that the biblical data he cites on religious conversion to Israel are demonstrably applicable to the recruitment of membership in earliest Israel. On narrow literary and historical grounds, his data are inapplicable to premonarchic Israel because they cannot be shown to be older than the eighth century B.C.E. at best. More tellingly, on broader socioreligious grounds, his data are inapplicable to premonarchic Israel because there exists the prima facie probability that there was a significant socioreligious structural and processual difference between "joining" Israel at its genesis and "joining" Israel once it had achieved a stable and continuing identity. "Conversion" will scarcely have meant the same thing in two such different stages of Israel's development.

The body of Milgrom's claims about conversion and assimilation in biblical Israel consists of an analysis of the P and D legislation on the topic, concerning which he concludes as follows:

1) Contrary to majority scholarly opinion, the Priestly writer treats the gēr in a legal status entirely separate from the Israelite. The gēr must keep only the prohibitive commandments, so as not to defile the holiness of land

and people, but need not keep the performative commandments incumbent on Israelites. Only Israelites were "full citizens" and there was no way provided by P, such as length of residency in the community or catechetical instruction, by which the *gēr* could pass into full citizenship.

2) Deuteronomy speaks about the imposition of *ḥērem* on the Canaanites (7:3) and the denial of admission to the *qāhāl* for bastards, Moabites and Ammonites (23:2-9). Taken together, the primary intent of these two provisions is to prevent intermarriage with any of the indigenous or neighboring peoples. D is worried that intermarriage with foreigners, far from assimilating them over time to the worship of Yahweh, will instead assimilate Israelites over time to the religion of the foreign spouses.

Surprisingly, Milgrom assumes without demonstration that these P and D stipulations were in force in premonarchic times and that it was only later, in postexilic times, that it became possible for gentiles to convert to Judaism in the sense of directly entering into the worship of Yahweh and enjoying at once the full rights of a Jewish citizen. It is taken for granted by Milgrom that premonarchic non-Israelites could only have been incorporated into Israel via the one route provided in P and D: marry an Israelite, keep a minimum of laws to safeguard holiness, and in time have their descendants become full Israelites. This appears to entail the further assumption that the holiness laws of P and D were observed centuries before the redaction of those legal collections. Furthermore, Milgrom perceives no distinction between individual gentiles converting and groups of gentiles converting, although he implicitly allows for group "assimilation."

By deduction from the foregoing premises, Milgrom is able to dismiss the construct of Israelite social revolutionary origins involving aggregations of "converts."

> Thus, the assumption of the revolt model that the national entity of Israel was formed by mass conversions to its covenantal faith is totally without warrant. . . . It [the assumption of mass conversion] is an anachronism, a gap of one thousand years. Conversion of individuals is not attested until the postexilic age, and the phenomenon of mass conversion not until the Hasmoneans and the advent of Christianity.[4]

Milgrom goes on to say that this anachronistic assumption of early mass conversions is "fatal" for Mendenhall's form of the revolutionary hypothesis since Israel was for Mendenhall—apart from the exodus Israelites—composed entirely of Canaanite converts. On the other hand, it is "less fatal," though still very damaging, to Gottwald's version of the revolutionary hypothesis because Gottwald allows for Canaanite "neutrals" (for example,

---

[4]Ibid., 175.

enclaves only later absorbed, such as Shechem and Jerusalem) and for Canaanite "allies" (for example, Gibeonites and Kenites). Therefore, what I proposed as "a secondary vehicle of absorption into Israel" was, in Milgrom's view, the exclusive way by which Canaanites could have become Israelites in early days: at first neutralized as a threat to Israel, they could assimilate over time through intermarriage with Israelites.

The net effect of Milgrom's critique is to expose what he judges to be a fundamental contradiction in the revolutionary model of early Israel. A viable model of Israelite origins must posit the preexisting ethnic unity of Israel from the start, since that is what P and D attest if they are read at face value with respect to premonarchic times. "But, if so," he asks, "in what sense will it be possible to ascribe the formation of Israel to a revolt?"[5] In short, Milgrom is able to account for Israel's initial composition only by the insertion of an extra-Canaanite ethnic entity whose process of emergence and formation he does *not* explore because it is assumed to lie anterior to the "entrance" of this "completed" people into the land. Since the revolutionary model *does* deliberately aim to explore the ethnic formation that Milgrom presupposes, and, moreover, to locate that formation *within the land itself*, it is clear that none of his objections pertain to those originative conditions in which Israelite self-identity was coming into being.

Surely we cannot accept P and D legislation as having been binding in premonarchic times without further ado. To be sure, it is widely believed that certain elements of P and D/Dtr preserve features from the tribal period. It is, in fact, critical to my own case for the revolutionary hypothesis that elements of Joshua and Judges, redacted by Dtr, give us clues to the originative formation of Israel which are at striking variance with the overall perspective of the final redaction. It is also my judgment that the tribal social organizational typology displayed in P yields valid information about premonarchic conditions, and in this I share a large measure of agreement with Milgrom who has elsewhere written on the topic."[6]

There is, however, no reason to give carte blanche credence to everything related or prescribed in P and D/Dtr. Each tradition must be independently evaluated, and, in the present instance, Milgrom does not show cause why P and D on "religious conversion" should be taken as reflective of premonarchic conditions.

Moreover, it is not alone the details of the instructions on the *gēr* and intermarriage which must be assessed, but also the overarching conception of

---

[5]Ibid., 176.

[6]Milgrom, "Priestly Terminology and the Political and Social Structure of Pre-Monarchic Israel," *JQR* 69 (1978): 65-81.

the social and religious whole envisioned in these retrospectively redacted documents which must be carefully weighed against the probable social realities of tribal times. The social locations of D/Dtr in late Judahite monarchic conditions of revival and collapse and of P in diaspora and restoration conditions were very different social settings from that of a decentralized coalition of tribal peoples struggling into existence. The commanding notion of tribal Israel as a unitary people already fully formed is constitutive of both D/Dtr, with its view of the tribal formation as a kind of proto-state, and of P, with its perception of the tribal union as a cult community in embryo. With disastrous results for the reconstruction of Israelite beginnings, biblical scholars have by and large taken over the D/Dtr conception of Israel as in principle a ''nation-state'' from the start. Marvin L. Chaney has driven home this sociopolitical blunder with telling effect:

> Proponents of the conquest model have been inconsistent and imprecise in conceptualizing Canaan, Israel, and their mutual antagonism. On the one hand, Canaan is understood to comprise various agrarian city-states with ever-shifting alliances and enmities, while Israel is envisaged as nomadic tribes, invading from the desert. At a more tacit level, however, following the lead of the ''Deuteronomistic Historian,'' the language used to speak of both seems to presuppose the nation-state as prototype . . . the nation-state in disguise. But if Canaan was a collection of jealous *city*-states, each with its own petty king, the *nation*-state mold fits premonarchic Israel even less well. Prior to its 13th century occupation of the hill country, it had no territorial definition; prior to David, its poor, unfortified towns and villages witness neither centralized political control nor the extraction and redistribution of a significant economic surplus. In short, the tenuous unity of premonarchic Israel, its lack of sharp social stratification, and its enmity for the city-states of Canaan cannot be explained by the tacit assumption of Israel's prior existence as a nation-state in the desert. The ''Deuteronomistic Historian'' and many moderns notwithstanding, the nation-state is not always the primary category of history.[7]

Thus, in naively positing premonarchic Israel as a virtual nation-state, Dtr reveals that it does not have the slightest conception of *a complex socioreligious process* by which Israel was formed, just as it lacks *a precisely documented historical account* of the events by which Israel came to power in Canaan. For D/Dtr, as likewise for P, the originative period of Israel is grasped fundamentally as a generative act of God rather than as an accomplishment of people in a particular social history.

---

[7]M. L. Chaney, ''Ancient Palestinian Peasant Movements and the Formation of Premonarchic Israel,'' *Palestine in Transition: The Emergence of Ancient Israel*, ed. D. N. Freedman and D. F. Graf (Sheffield: Almond, 1983) 47-48.

For Dtr to manifest this kind of sociohistorical "blind spot" is of course entirely understandable, but it is another matter when biblical scholars, who have access to sociological method and theory, perpetuate Dtr's misperception. Consequently, whatever the merits of Milgrom's textual exegesis, which for the purposes of this paper need not be contested nor confirmed, his attempt to "translate" the results into an assessment of the circumstances of Israel's initial formation must be judged a failure. Fundamentally it is a failure because it mismatches data from *very different social worlds* when it tries to transplant recruitment or conversion criteria from the *nation-state* social construct of D and the *cult-community* social construct of P into the social world of the *associated tribes* of nascent Israel.

The social revolutionary notion of "mass conversion" in early Israel is not really, as Milgrom claims, a "tacit assumption," since its adherents set it forth as an open hypothesis. There is, however, a deep-rooted tacit assumption behind this hypothesis, as is the case with all the other hypotheses involved in the social revolutionary model, and it runs like this: without exception, everything told us in the Bible about Israel's origins is set forth in late redactional frames that give an airily religious version of Israel's beginnings which must be thoroughly "deconstructed" and "reconstructed" into a social historical rendering of human activities.

With respect to the "conversion" theme at hand, as with all other features of Israel's origins, we must posit Israel as a sociohistorical phenomenon that at one time did not exist and then, under particular circumstances, did come into being, at first as loosely linked tribes and eventually as a state. We have much clearer information as to how the Israelite state arose than we possess concerning the emergence of the associated tribes whose beginnings were largely preliterate. The biblical account is essentially folkloric in its format and tone, even when we allow for a greater "history-like" aspect in parts of its "filler" traditions.

This highly schematic traditional account tells us that Israel arose through a call to one man and his family which through natural propagation grew to be twelve tribes that entered Canaan from Egypt and conquered the land. The vast majority of scholars concur that this is an artificial construct that does not bear up under scrutiny, for a host of reasons. In this regard Israel's origin stories are much like others the world over that cast the obscure beginnings of a people eponymously in terms of the actions of single persons and small groups that are genealogically related. Often these folkish origin stories leave unexplained gaps in the narration and switch the locale or scope of the subject without clear transition signals. All these features of popular origin stories defy the recognized canons of descriptive history writing.[8]

---

For example, consider the hiatus between the end of Genesis where Israel consists of the seventy-odd folk in Jacob's family and the beginning of Exodus where Israelite slaves are "swarming" in their thousands, to the extent that they terrify pharaoh as a threat to Egyptian rule. Add to this the decided evidence from many sources that by no means all Israelites in Canaan, or even a majority of them, were escapees from Egypt. All in all, as Martin Noth's pentateuchal analysis underscored conclusively—however we may dispute him on particulars—the stylized format of the origin themes gives us full justification to focus our attempts to reconstruct Israelite origins on the incremental growth of Israel in Canaan.[9]

From the standpoint of "Israel forming within Canaan," we are best positioned to approach the patriarchal and exodus tradition complexes from the proper perspective, reading them "backward" as it were, since they appear to function primarily as dramatic "root metaphors" which tell us mainly about the vital formative processes and concerns of the highland Israelites. It is probably also the case that these patriarchal and exodus tradition complexes contain valid memories about the fortunes of certain groups who entered into the formation of Israel. The very possibility of extracting such information from them, however, depends upon our first establishing them firmly as literary retrojections produced by Israel as it took shape in Canaan.

For the purposes of our discussion about conversion in early Israel, the preceding understanding of the genesis of the origin traditions is of decisive importance. I am convinced that it is a methodological and epistemological error of major proportions to attribute to "Israel" of the patriarchal and exodus traditions a "completed" and "cohesive" ethnicity which was simply extended unaltered into tribal Israel.

Consequently, behind this "family tree" image of Israel's birth, with the sons of Jacob spawning the closely knit tribes of Israel conceived as a family writ large, we are searching for sociohistoric conjunctures of peoples, and of conditions and processes, that can best explain how Israel came about, if only by initially *delimiting possibilities* and *excluding improbabilities*. This "explanation" by delimitation and exclusion must include a clarification of Israel's peculiar "tribalism," which we can no longer attribute simply to a prolongation of pastoral nomadism, but must grasp and explicate as some-

---

[8]For an important methodological discussion, based mainly on African examples, see J. Vansina, *Oral Tradition as History* (Madison: University of Wisconsin, 1985) especially 21-24.

[9]M. Noth, *A History of Pentateuchal Traditions* (Englewood Cliffs: Prentice-Hall, 1972) 42-45, 252-59.

thing more akin to a "revitalization movement."[10] This "explanation" must also include an integral, socially critical reading of the rich body of literary traditions which speaks so eloquently of a complex socioreligious process of popular formation.

At this point the comparative study of Israel's origin stories in relation to the origin stories of various peoples the world over is a most needful and promising research task. This is so because in certain respects, and from case to case, we are more knowledgeable about the genesis of these peoples than we are of the genesis of Israel. Within our grasp is the possibility of controlled comparisons that specify the ways in which the formation of Israel may be judged comparable, and thus be significantly enlightened by, for example, the formation of the Icelandic, Iroquois or Sioux peoples. By the nature of all the variables involved in such far-flung and diverse social constellations, these comparisons will be delimitations of possibilities and probabilities rather than one-to-one proofs.[11] In a situation, however, where even though the biblical text and the archaeological data are exhaustively combed for new ideas, various competing explanations of Israelite origins continue in stalemate, such comparative inquiry into the origin stories of known peoples is a largely untapped resource of incalculable worth.

To give but one example, it strikes me as more and more evident that while we cannot yet give a very confident assessment of the historical veracity of the Egyptian sojourn and exodus traditions, we can say quite a bit in terms of the social referents and allusions of those traditions, provided that we understand that those referents and allusions are in the first instance grounded in social conditions in highland Canaan. It is plausible, perhaps even compelling, to recognize in the traditional "portraits" of Moses and the other Israelite leaders definite projections of the type of bicultural risk-takers who, like the "intellectuals of the new order" vital to the leadership of peasant movements in our time,[12] were the "brains" that joined with the "muscles" of the Israelite rank and file to devise flexible strategies and tactics for building the tribal confederacy as a viable way of life.

The conception of Israel's formation crucial to my argument is that premonarchic Israel was a people composing itself cumulatively by a new bond-

---

[10]The programmatic essay on this topic is A. F. C. Wallace, "Revitalization Movements," *American Anthropologist* 58 (1956): 264-81. In studies of ancient Israel, apart from my *Tribes of Yahweh*, "revitalization" concepts have been chiefly applied to prophecy and apocalyptic. See *Semeia* 21 (1982) devoted to "Anthropological Perspectives on OT Prophecy" (ed. R. C. Culley and T. W. Overholt).

[11]R. R. Wilson, *Sociological Approaches to the OT* (Philadelphia: Fortress, 1984), 28-29.

[12]E. R. Wolf, *Peasant Wars of the Twentieth Century* (New York: Harper & Row, 1969) 287-89.

ing of individuals and groups, all of whom were leaving previous allegiances
and identities as they developed their new Israelite identity. Thus it is evident
that my actual "tacit assumption" about "conversion" in premonarchic Israel is very different than Milgrom supposes. I do not assume that early Israel
received outsiders into an already very well defined community that in its essential structures and practices was like the community of Israel in later centuries. Nor do I assume that transfer of loyalties to the Israelite community in
early days was preeminently for religious reasons in analogy with postexilic
conversions to Judaism. In fact, we make no progress in reconstructing Israel's origins as long as we assume close equivalence between social and religious terms in earliest Israel and in later Israel.

Stated positively, my tacit assumption is to expect Israel's originative socioreligious formation to have differed considerably from its later maturing
formation, so that all considerations of what it meant to "be" Israelite and to
"join" Israel in the two situations must be formulated carefully with full regard for the differing socioreligious contexts. Working out of this assumption, my hypothesis is that Israel was formed in Canaan out of a number of
elements of the populace, with differing degrees and kinds of previous identities, and that the "Israel" so formed was not only, or even chiefly, a religious community but an entire social formation, a whole socioeconomic and
cultural system, which simultaneously developed a religion of prominence as
one major component in the forging of group identity.

Very likely "conversion" is a misleading word for the premonarchic
context.[13] "Recruitment" and "commitment" to a risky social project come
closer to demarcating the community-building process through which Israel
arose. In fact, I did not make much use of the term "conversion" in *The Tribes
of Yahweh*, and when I did employ it in one of my key formulations, I put it
in quotation marks:

> As to the mode of Canaanite "conversion" to Israel, I have in mind
> situations wherein city-state rulers and upper classes are overthrown, thereby
> freeing elements of the city-state populace to incorporate in the burgeoning
> alternative social system of Israel.[14]

"Conversion" ( = recruitment/commitment) in this instance meant entering
a social movement that was tending toward a societal formation with its own
growing coherence and distinction. To "enter" this movement as a society-
in-the-making was to participate in resistance to taxing and conscripting sov-

---

[13]L. R. Rambo, "Current Research on Religious Conversion," *RSR* 8 (1982): 146-59,
provides an extensive bibliographic survey of recent anthropological, sociological, historical,
psychological, psychoanalytic and theological studies.

[14]Gottwald, *Tribes*, 556.

ereignties and, as the necessary corollary of that resistance, to participate in the building of networks of self-help and self-understanding to replace the rejected "social services" and "cultural interpretations" of city-state organization and ideology.

The primary vehicle in early Israel for providing a new cultural self-understanding was the religion of Yahweh. The formerly powerless of Canaan (the "no people") were becoming powerful enough to control their lives as never before (at last "a people," "the people of Yahweh"). Clearly then religion played a part in these initial conversion-recruitments to Israelite ranks, but we must not be too quick to assume the content or social placement of Yahwism in that formative period. In particular, we must avoid the assumption which Milgrom appears to make, namely, that the shifts in commitments and loyalties involved in the world of Israelite identity-in-the-making are to be equated, even roughly, with those involved in the world of a long-developed Israelite-Jewish identity.

In considering conversion as participation in the originative formation of Israel, we must recognize that this initial Israelite movement and social formation was not a religion or religious group within the categories of a "church"/"sect" typology, that is, a religious folk who share social, political and cultural features secondarily or peripherally to their fundamental and separately constituted religious identity. The religious language of early Israelite self-understanding should not deceive us into abstracting and segregating the religion from the total social and cultural formation. The religion of early Israel must be viewed in its sociocultural embededness, whether as a cultural subset or as the symbolic and ritual dimension of the whole culture, for it can be viewed fruitfully from both perspectives. Religious talk and practice in early Israel were emphatic functions of social struggle:

> In Israel the object of the divine activity is an entire people struggling
> to unify and defend a living space on the organizational principle of equal
> access to the basic resources for all members.[15]

The capacity to hold religion firmly within its largest social and cultural matrix, denying it independent causative or metaphysical privilege in our historical analysis, is easier to sustain in studying religions other than our own. For this reason, comparative study of non-Jewish and non-Christian socioreligious phenomena, including conversion, is likely to be resisted as irrelevant for early Israel at the very juncture where it is most needed to "open up" our understanding.

The anthropologist Robin Horton, who has extensively studied the circumstances and conditions of African conversions to Islam and Christian-

---

[15]Ibid., 697. For the meaning of egalitarianism as applied to early Israel, see 798-99n635.

ity,[16] has some cogent things to say about the "theological chauvinism" with which some Christian historians and anthropologists have responded to his conclusions. Horton studied the relationship between African native beliefs in high gods and lesser gods, on the one hand, and the incidence of conversions to Islam and Christianity, on the other hand. He concluded that conversions to these monotheistic missionizing religions were most frequent and abiding when the sociohistoric situation had already prompted a shift in the focus of attention within the native beliefs and rituals away from the lesser gods, who deal with immediate details of life, toward the normally more remote high gods, who deal with those larger problems of the society which emerge urgently in times of change or crisis. In other words, a predilection toward Islamic/Christian monotheism was spurred by large-scale social systemic change and threat mediated through the monotheizing tendencies in the native religions.

The response of some Christian scholars to this argument was to hold resolutely to the position that religion alone can explain the conversions and, more specifically, that "true religion," in this case Christianity, is not amenable to non-religious explanations. Horton called these critics of his position, which included Edward Evans-Pritchard and Victor Turner, "The Devout Opposition."[17] In the judgment of these opponents of sociohistoric explanation of religious effects, African preparation for and conversion to Islam or Christianity should be interpreted in terms of theological or ecclesial triumphalism. In their thinking, Horton claims, the genetic fallacy is alive and well: if you can explain how deeply religion has been mixed with and moved by secular factors, you thereby weaken religion or show it to be false. Horton sums up Evans-Pritchard's way of sealing off "true religion," and its pagan anticipations, from radical sociohistorical inquiry:

> . . . causal explanation is appropriate to illusory beliefs, but not to true ones.
> For the Christian, all beliefs in spiritual reality, whether monotheistic or
> polytheistic, are at least approximations to the truth. Hence it is fruitless to
> search for their causal antecedents.[18]

In terms of our inquiry into conversion in early Israel, "devout opposition" to a social critical interpretation of Israelite faith sometimes takes the

---

[16]R. Horton, "African Conversion," *Journal of the International African Institute* 41 (1971): 85-108, and "On the Rationality of Conversion," *Journal of the International African Institute* 45 (1975): 219-35, 373-98.

[17]Horton, "On the Rationality of Conversion," 394-97. . In sharp contrast to Horton's "devout oppositionists," A. R. Tippett, without recourse to spiritual or theological causes, schematizes the conversion process to Christianity in Oceania with anthropological and sociological sophistication: "Conversion as a Dynamic Process in Christian Mission," *Missiology* 5 (1977): 203-21.

[18]Ibid., 396.

direct form of assertions about the privileged and therefore socially unana-
lyzable priority of the revealed truth of the biblical account. More often,
however, the opposition appears in the form of assumptions about Israel as
"an unchanging essence" or about Israel's faith as "transcending history."
Whatever rough-hewn symbolic value these assertions may have, as mind-
sets they contribute to half-hearted and inconsistent application of historical
method when the sacred history-transcending categories are substituted for
rigorous social-historical thinking. Although Milgrom does not address these
assumptions, and it would thus be inaccurate of me to attribute them to him,
it does seem to me that his reluctance or resistance to conceptualizing early
Israel in a processual mode rests logically on such essentialist views of biblical Israel. And because this basic orientation is not unique to Milgrom, but
is evident in the work of many biblical scholars, it is important that it be sur-
faced for critical consideration if the day-to-day work of biblical studies is to
be clarified and prospered.

If we turn for a moment to consider what did happen in the formation of
Israel out of diverse preexistent identities, two issues, prompted by the work
of Milgrom and Horton, deserve to be formulated and briefly commented on:
1) insofar as the religion of Yahweh was but one subset of Israelite society,
once a cult of Yahweh became the dominant unifying religious force, by what
means did newcomers to Israel enter into the formalities of the cult?; 2) since
a "new" religion always draws in some measure on features of older religions, and may even be precipitated by elements of the older religions which
are suddenly depreciated or brought to prominence in a radically altered way,
what are the possible "triggers" in Canaanite religion which may have contributed to the eruption of Yahwism in Israel?

Over against spiritualizing abstractions that remove Israel's religion from
its social matrix, I have consistently stressed the close fit between religious
identity and sociopolitical identity in early Israel. To be or to become Israelite
was to acknowledge Yahweh and at the same time it was to be part of or to
enter into a movement of decentralized villagers bent on overthrowing the
tributary rule of city-states in the region. To become Israelite was to make a
break and to reorient religiously and sociopolitically with life and death stakes.

Nonetheless, internally the "fit" between religion and sociopolitical
reality was hardly a simple harmonious one. It appears that Yahwism had to
win its way in Israelite circles against considerable hostility and apathy. It
also appears that the vanguard Levites formed a propagandizing and organiz-
ing cadre for the propagation and consolidation of Yahwism. When this uphill
battle of the new cult is taken into account, it is likely that allowance should
be made for the possibility that in some cases, varying perhaps by region and
over time, people who entered Israel were "on probation," even if that meant
no more than that their participation in the cult was approved by Levites after

a suitable period of instruction. In that event, people newly joined to Israel might already be socially a part of Israel and militarily active in its defense before they satisfied all the requirements for participation in the cult. Certain features of the incorporating ceremonies (covenants) in Joshua 9 and 24 may best be understood on the model of probation for newcomers to the religion of Yahweh.

To be sure, consideration of continuities and discontinuities between Canaanite and Israelite religion, along the lines of Horton's exploration of the move from African native faiths to Islam and Christianity, is greatly hampered by minimal evidence as to how the Canaanite cults operated in the lives of those mainly rural highland people who became Israelites.[19] Looking at the decisive sociohistoric pressures on religion, what "filters" would have operated for retaining or rejecting Canaanite religious belief or practice and what impetuses would have encouraged adoption of a new cult?

Israel took shape as an agrarian society that before all else had to master highland cultivation in order to take root and survive. Secondly, it had to be able to defend itself against city-state sovereignties that attempted to dominate it. Thirdly, it had to develop internal self-rule and self-help procedures in order to serve the collective interests of its members. Lastly, it had to develop a way of understanding itself that could be articulated in religious symbols and rituals. How did the first three needs influence the adoptions and adaptations in religion?

It seems that the religious dilemma facing this new social movement was not an easy one to resolve. The Canaanite "high gods" were tied into the city-state system as an ideological support for the hegemony Israel was rejecting. The cults of the Canaanite "lesser gods," presumably the main preoccupation of agrarians, would appeal to the Israelite insurgents as the received sensible practice for cultivators of the soil. The dilemma was two-fold: the aspects of Canaanite religion that would prosper Israelite agriculture and the aspects of Canaanite religion that would justify city-state dominion and delegitimate the Israelite social project were so closely linked that they could not be easily separated. It would be difficult "to pick and choose" among the Canaanite religious offerings without in one way or another "buying into" their ideological function in buttressing city-state rule over the countryside.

What was needed was a religion that would prosper agriculture and underwrite a communitarian mode of life. Whatever its source, the cult of Yahweh came to meet this need, but only it seems through a complex dialectical contest with Canaanite religion. Yahwism resolved the dilemma by provid-

---

[19]N. Gottwald, "Early Israel and the Canaanite Socioeconomic System," in *Palestine in Transition*, 32-33, questions whether the theocratic ideology of Canaanite state religion succeeded in permeating popular culture with a common world view.

ing a deity who was equally concerned both to deliver his people from tributary dominion to communitarian freedom and to prosper them in their arduous
struggle to extract their livelihood from the highland soil. It appears, however, that Yahweh had been in the first instance the deity of deliverance from
oppressive circumstances and only secondarily a god of fertility. Consequently, the challenge for Israel, and especially for the Levitical devotees and
interpreters of this god, was to make firm the link between the history-mak-
ing and nature-fecundating aspects of Yahweh, and to do this in such a way
as to renounce religious legitimation for Canaanite politics and social strati-
fication.

In this process of sorting out the religious *old* and the religious *new*, the
generic name for the Canaanite "father god," El, was retained as one of Yahweh's names, while the name Baal, more threatening because of his apparently closer association with agrarian cults, was rejected. Many of the
particulars of Canaanite religion, from its mode of producing religious songs
to its sacrificial system, were easily preserved by the Israelite movement as
long as they could be shorn of their ideological support of the Canaanite city-
state. Looked at in terms of resolving a fundamental dilemma in the tension
between religion and social structure, the curious twists and turns by which
Israel both appropriated and rejected Canaanite religion are more understandable than when viewed solely as religious choices.[20] It is also clear that no
once and for all clear-cut decisions in these religious matters could be counted
on to prevail, inasmuch as the Levites and the most loyal Yahweh adherents
had to rely mainly on example and persuasion since, as a decentralized pol-
ity, there was no way to compel compliance in a lasting manner.

In conclusion, Milgrom makes one specific objection to the revolutionary hypothesis which merits response because it is a recurrent one among critics of the hypothesis. The objection may be broadly phrased in this way: Israel
could not have originated in social revolution because its traditions preserve
no explicit or incontestable memory of such a social revolution.

Milgrom's form of that objection is couched in this manner: "A mass
conversion of Canaanites during Israel's formative period would not have been

---

[20] D. R. Hillers, "Analyzing the Abominable: Our Understanding of Canaanite Religion," *JQR* 75 (1985): 253-69, faults *Tribes* for a moralistic negative view of Canaanite religion essentially no different than the judgmental view of the older "biblical theology"
advocates. Hillers appears not to have attended closely to my assessment of Israelite theology
as a development within a shared ancient Near Eastern "common theology" (see n24 below),
and, in particular, he has overlooked my extended dialogue with the views of "the Cross school"
and W. Brueggemann on the error of nature-history dualism in evaluating Canaanite and Israelite religions as polar opposites pure and simple (*Tribes*, 903-13). Although compressed,
D. Sperling has an excellent sketch of the Canaanite-Israelite religious dialectic as a dimension
of Israel's formative social revolution ("Israel's Religion in the Ancient Near East," *Jewish
Spirituality*, ed. A. Green [New York: Crossroad, 1986] 5-31).

ignored by Deuteronomy.''[21] Strictly speaking, Milgrom is correct. Had Deuteronomy known of such a phenomenon, it would have been worked into the book in some way, possibly as a one-time exception for incorporating supposedly sincere Canaanites no longer to be allowed because the undertaking had not worked out well.

If, however, the overarching interpretive framework of Deuteronomy does not go back with any certainty beyond the eighth century, why should we think that the actual circumstances of Israel's emergence in Canaan would any longer be clearly remembered in their unique totality? This was, however, not simply a memory ''fade-out'' over three or four centuries. Major changes in society that are later overturned or reversed tend to be forgotten. We can see quite definite reasons for this ''forgetting'' in the case of Israel. It was certainly in the interests of those who profited from the reversal of Israel's social revolution to erase that memory insofar as possible.

In fact, the subsequent development of Israelite traditions can be viewed as a contest between those who sought to erase the memories of social revolution and those who sought to preserve and rekindle those memories. The former, commanding as they did substantial political power and literary resources, were able to obscure the memories of social revolution, but they did not succeed in expunging them altogether because the revolutionary roots of Israel lived on in the hearts and minds of others who were able to maintain and nourish aspects of the original communitarian practice within the social infrastructure that resisted the encroachments of monarchic administration and ideology.

After two centuries, Israel became a single monarchic state and then split into two states. Centralized governments require unequivocal stability and solid historical charters. Monarchic Israelite circles derived the state-charter from God via the patriarchs, Moses and Joshua, eventually to be actualized in the dynasty of David. The writers and keepers of the literary traditions were chiefly those under state aegis. To have retained and cultivated the social revolutionary specifics of Israel's beginnings would have been to place the security of the Israelite monarchy in jeopardy, since a people that began in social revolution might turn revolutionary against their own kings, and in fact such did happen more than once, although these outbursts against royal authority were always subsequently contained within yet another centralized dynastic structure. When one considers how much of the social revolutionary thrust and potential of American history has been ''forgotten'' over two hundred years of time, even though those tendencies are fully documented, it should not surprise us that the circumstances and the basic process of Israel's originative social revolution were lost to view.

---

[21]Milgrom, ''Religious Conversion,'' 173.

Since earliest Israel was a folk movement struggling to establish itself under adverse and spartan conditions, it seems that the main tradition-building energy went into serving the immediate needs of the new society by means of liturgies and laws rather than into relating the past by means of connected accounts of how the revolution took place. There were narratives no doubt, portions of which survive in Dtr, but these narratives seem to have been recited at cultic celebrations and thus were never given a larger historical context. By the time monarchic traditionists attempted to provide a larger context, the older narratives had lost their revolutionary edge, either through modification at the oral stage or in editing by pre-Deuteronomic collectors. Moreover, since during the monarchy the defense requirements of Israel were met by a professional army under state command, a social context no longer existed for the practice of military initiative by a citizen militia which had been the backbone of Israel's formative social revolution. Therefore, as Milgrom observes, it is doubtful that Dtr knew of any comprehensive social revolutionary scenario in which to lodge the older stories, even though some aspects of that scenario might have been serviceable to the nationalist restoration of Josiah had Dtr known of it.

Those who, like Milgrom, protest that the origin stories lack revolutionary memory need to be reminded that, when it comes to describing the actual circumstances of Israel's formation in Canaan, the origin stories do not preserve *any single coherent perspective* on the spatiotemporal process. The so-called Dtr framework of Joshua is shot through with vague generalities that naively retroject united Israel as a nation-state in arms. The Dtr framework does not display Israel as a socially articulated people, beyond the twelve-tribe device, and does not register a military strategy nor show a sequence of victories. Strictly speaking the commanding Dtr outlook does not present a developed historically plausible account of "conquest," "immigration" or "social revolution." It is only in the diverse "filler" traditions used by Dtr that we find scattered social organizational and military data which require us to assemble them into a reconstruction of events, structures and processes in one form or another. In short, the social revolutionary hypothesis labors under no greater disadvantage than all hypotheses about Israelite origins in the land. "Conquest" or "immigration" only appear to be more valid models because they have been dominant in biblical scholarship and because the monarchic apologists worked so successfully to exclude "social revolution" as an interpretive option.

But, although Israel's originative social revolution is lost as an interpretive frame for reporting the overall process of its establishment in Canaan, the impact and effects of that social revolution show up in many other ways. For example, if Robert Polzin is correct, even in the subtext of Dtr's redaction of Joshua and Judges there is a stress on the disquieting incorporation of "outsiders" into early Israel which may indirectly preserve displaced recollections of Israel's formation out of "mixed peoples."[22]

Most significantly, although the precise course of the social revolution that birthed Israel is not described in the Bible, many of the norms and practices of the newly formed society are reported, even if offhandedly and piecemeal for the most part, in all the major blocs of biblical literature, ranging through song, narrative, law, wisdom, prophecy and apocalyptic.[23] Furthermore, that which distinguished the religion of Yahweh from "the common theology" of the ancient Near East with which it shared so much (as Morton Smith and Bertil Albrektson have convincingly demonstrated), is precisely a theological and ethical gestalt correspondent with communitarian values and practices in opposition to hierarchic privileges and controls.[24]

Thus it is not a mere matter of locating "fossils" of the originative social revolution in Joshua and Judges, but it is also a matter of identifying persisting communitarian norms and practices in the infrastructure of Israelite society and religion in subsequent periods, even though these norms and practices were overdetermined by hierarchic rule. There is good reason to believe that the founding Israelite impulse to be self-determining and self-producing contributed to Jewish survival in exile and dispersion under colonial conditions, as also to the confrontation with Hellenistic and Roman overlords and their Jewish collaborators, and finally to the hardy grass roots character of rabbinic Judaism.[25]

---

[22]R. Polzin, *Moses and the Deuteronomist. A Literary Study of the Deuteronomic History* (New York: Seabury, 1980) 124-45.

[23]Chaney, "Ancient Palestinian Peasant Movements," 67-72; H. E. von Waldow, "Social Responsibility and Social Structure in Early Israel," *CBQ* 32 (1970): 182-204.

[24]Gottwald, *Tribes*, 670-91; see also n20 above.

[25]Gottwald, *The Hebrew Bible—A Socio-Literary Introduction* (Philadelphia: Fortress, 1985) 419-56.

# THE REDACTION
# OF EZRA 4-6:
# A PLEA FOR
# A THEOLOGY OF SCRIBES

HANS H.-MALLAU
BAPTIST THEOLOGICAL SEMINARY
RÜSCHLIKON SWITZERLAND CH-8803

## 1. MANY PROBLEMS AND NO SOLUTIONS.

The Aramaic texts in Ezra 4:8-6:18 and their Hebrew frame in Ezra 4:1-7 and 6:19-22 have posed difficulties since the time of ancient interpreters. We can outline a few of these problems:

a) The combination of (1) the "temple reconstruction crisis" in the times of the Persian kings Cyrus (B.C. [558] 538-530) and Darius (B.C. [522-486] 520-515)[1] with (2) letters between Palestine state officers and the Persian kings Xerxes (B.C. 485-465)[2] and Artaxerxes (B.C. 464-424)[3] on the problem of the fortification of the city of Jerusalem is anachronistic.

b) The fact that the "documents" from the time of Xerxes and Artaxerxes are placed before those of the time of Darius[4] contradicts the chronological

---

[1]Ezra 4:1-5, 24.

[2]Ezra 4:6.

[3]Ezra 4:11-22.

[4]Ezra 5:6-6:12.

structure of the narrative, which places the temple reconstruction crisis[5] before the completion and dedication of the temple.[6]

c) The "documents" deal with two different problems: the fortification of the city of Jerusalem[7] and the reconstruction of the Temple.[8]

d) The double reference to the interruption of construction work on the temple, alternately caused by the "people of the land"[9] and by the state officials involved in the correspondence with king Artaxerxes, is historically problematic.[10]

e) The use of the Aramaic language not only for quotations from "documents" but also for the narratives framing these documents;[11] the unabridged combination of a quotation from Persian archive materials[12] with a letter of king Darius to Tatnai, governor of Transeuphrates;[13] and the different wordings of the "edict of Cyrus" in repeated quotations[14] provoke doubts in the trustworthiness of the "Aramaic documents" and give rise to various interpretations of the nature of the Aramaic sections of the book of Ezra.

Ancient authors tried to solve some of these problems. The apocryphal book "1 Esdras"[15] has restructured the texts of Ezra 4-6.[16] It has added a new

---

[5]Ezra 4:1-5, 23f.

[6]Ezra 6:13-22. The traditional assumption that the authors or redactors may not have known the correct sequence of Persian kings creates new problems. Not only would the correct sequence Cyrus-Darius-Artaxerxes of Ezra 6:14 need an explanation, but even more problematic would be why Zerubbabel and Jeshua had dared to take up the temple reconstruction while there existed a royal decree forbidding it (Ezra 4:[23] 24); it is also quite surprising that there is no mention of this decree in the subsequent negotiations between the elders of Judah and governor Tatnai on the legitimacy of the temple reconstruction (Ezra 5:3ff.).

[7]Ezra 4:11-22 (23).

[8]Ezra 5:7-6:12.

[9]Ezra 4:5.

[10]Ezra 4:23 (24).

[11]Ezra 4:8, 17a, 23-24; 5:1-7a; 6:1-2, 13-18.

[12]Ezra 6:3-5.

[13]Ezra 6:6ff.

[14] 2 Chr 26:23; Ezra 1:2-4; 6:3-5.

[15] 3 Esra according to German tradition; probably a late 2nd century B.C. writing. Recent translation into German: Karl-Friedrich Pohlmann, "3 Esra-Buch," in *Jüdische Schriften aus hellenistisch-römisher Zeit*, ed. W. G. Kümmel (Gütersloh: Mohn, 1980) 1:375-425.

[16] 1 Esdr separated the Artaxerxes correspondence (Ezra 4:11-22 = 1 Esdr 2:15-25) from the temple reconstruction crisis (Ezra 4:1-5 = 1 Esdr 5:63-70) and from the subsequent report on the temple building activities under king Darius (Ezra 5:1-6:22 = 1 Esdr 6:1-7:15) but most problems have remained unsolved.

story about Zerubbabel's wisdom and merit,[17] and it evades the problem of the transition from Hebrew to Aramaic in the biblical book of Ezra by utilizing only Greek. On the other hand 1 Esdras creates new problems[18] and other problems remain unsolved.[19] Josephus,[20] using both the Biblical and the apocryphal Ezra material,[21] completed the reconciliation between the different topics of Ezra 4-6.[22]

Recent historical-critical investigation has added an uncounted number of suggestions to solve the difficulties of Ezra 4-6. Unfortunately there is no recent study available on the present state of research.[23] However, it is quite apparent that the majority of the above mentioned problems has remained unsolved. The old controversy on the authenticity of the quoted documents[24] is still disputed.[25] A tiring repetition of arguments has still not yielded any agreement as to whether the book of Ezra is a continuation of the books of Chronicles,[26] or if the use of the Aramaic language is due to a separate literary

---

[17] 1 Esdr 3-4. In the wisdom dispute of young men before Darius, Serubbabel, being one of them, is the winner of the argument and uses the opportunity to speak to king Darius and to change his mind concerning the Jerusalem temple.

[18] There are references to the reconstruction of the temple inserted in the Artaxerxes correspondence (1 Esdr 2:17-18).

[19] E.g., why this correspondence precedes the reconstruction of the temple in the days of Darius (Ezra 4:24 = 1 Esdr 2:25).

[20] Ant. 11.1.2ff.

[21] For Josephus' use of 1 Esdr see Karl-Friedrich Pohlmann, *Studien zum 3. Esra*, FRLANT 104 (Göttingen: Vandenhoeck, 1970) 74ff.

[22] He inserts the royal permission to reconstruct the city of Jerusalem into the edict of Cyrus (Ant 11.1.2f.) and finally even repairs the chronological problem by changing the name of Artaxerxes to Cambyses (B.C. 530-522), the successor to the throne of Cyrus.

[23] There are extensive bibliographies in the recent commentaries of H. G. M. Williamson, *Ezra, Nehemiah* vol. 16 of *Word Biblical Commentary* (Waco: 1985): xviii-xx; and Antonius H. J. Gunneweg, *Esra,* KAT (Gütersloh: Mohn, 1985): 32-39.

[24] Eduard Meyer, *Die Entstehung des Judentums* (Halle: 1896) had defended the authenticity of these documents in opposition to J. Wellhausen, *Die Rückkehr der Juden aus dem babylonischen Exil, Nachrichten von der königlichen Gesellschaft der Wissenschaften zu Göttingen* (1985) 166-86; and W. H. Kosters, *Het Herstel van Israel in het Perzische Tijdvak* (1893) 28-30, 63-74; while C. C. Torrey, *The Composition and Historical Value of Ezra-Nehemiah,* BZAW, 2 (Giessen: 1896) 5ff. & 55ff., and more elaborately in *Ezra Studies,* KTAV (New York: 1970=1910) 140-207, has argued that the Aramaic sections of the book of Ezra were composed by a middle third century author, contemporary and related to the school of the Chronicler.

[25] See the above mentioned commentaries (n23) of Antonius H. J. Gunneweg, 85ff., who pleads for an original Aramaic chronicle which does not contain any authentic historical source material, and H. G. M. Williamson, xxiiiff. who continues to presuppose authentic historical documents.

[26] See the discussion of linguistic arguments in recent literature and the disillusioning con-

source[27] or to the literary intentions of one Biblical writer.[28] The list of open questions may be continued *ad libitum*. This stalemate of recent research invites us to concentrate on additional observations with the acknowledgment that they may also fail to solve every problem.

## 2. THE PARALLEL COMPOSITION OF EZRA 4 AND EZRA 5-6

The parallel structure and the paradigmatic contrasts of the two texts are just as noteworthy as other elements which do not fit into this structure. Elements of the plot are:[29]

| | | | | | |
|---|---|---|---|---|---|
| 1. | 4:1-3 | Conflict<br>Reconstruction of temple<br>(details do not reappear in<br>letters) [*hekal le-yahweh*] | 5:1-4 | Conflict<br>Reconstruction of temple<br>(details reappear in letters)<br>[*bet 'elaha'*] |
| 2. | 4:4-5 | Consequence<br>building activity is stopped | 5:5 | Consequence<br>building activity continues |
| a) | 4:6 | (anonymous?) Written accusation (*sitnah*) against Judah and Jerusalem, addressed to Xerxes. Content of letter is missing | | |
| b) | 4:7 | Letter (*ništewan*) of Bishlam, Mithredath, Tabeel, and others to Artaxerxes. Content of letter is missing (end of Hebrew text) | | |
| 3. | 4:8-11 | Copy (*paršegen*) of letter (*'iggera'*) of Rehum and Shimshai and others to Artaxerxes | 5:6-7 | Copy (*paršegen*) of letter (*'iggera'*) of Tattenai and Shetar-bozenai and others to Darius |
| 4. | 4:12 | Situation: Jews are rebuilding the city of Jerusalem | 5:8 | Situation: (Jews) are rebuilding the temple of Jerusalem |

---

clusion that "linguistic analysis is (not) capable of providing definite proof either way," in Mark A. Throntveit, "Linguistic Analysis of the Questions of Authorship in Chronicles, Ezra, and Nehemiah," *VT* 32 (1982): 201-16; again the recent commentaries of Gunneweg (24ff. arguing for a continued literary context), and Williamson (xxxiiiff., arguing against it) take alternative positions.

[27]So Gunneweg, "Die aramäische und hebräische Erzählung über die nachexilische Restauration—ein Vergleich," *ZAW* 94 (1982): 299-302 (see also above, see n24).

[28]See Daniel C. Snell, "Why is there Aramaic in the Bible," *JSOT* 18 (1980): 32-51.

[29]Parallel (and contrasting) elements are marked with numbers, while contradictory elements and those without parallel are marked with letters.

| | | | | |
|---|---|---|---|---|
| 5. | 4:13f. | Warning of consequences: threat to Persian empire | 5:9-16 | Information about debate with elders: obedience to the edict of king Cyrus |
| 6. | 4:15 | Recommendation to search (*bqr, pe*) royal archives (*sefar dokranayya'*) to confirm the warnings of the writers | 5:17a | Recommendation to search (*bqr, hitp*) royal archives of Babel (*bet gizrayya'*) to confirm the argument of Jewish elders |
| 7. | 4:16 | Renewed warning of consequences if reconstruction continues | 5:17b | Expectation of unprejudiced royal answer |
| c) | | | 6:1-5 | problems of Darius' successful search (the document is finally found at Ecbatana); text of document (*dikronah*) |
| 8. | 4:17-22 | Response (*pitgama'*) of Artaxerxes | 6:6-12 | Response of Darius |
| d) | | | 6:6 | No introduction of letter |
| 9. | 4:19-20 | Archives confirm warnings of the writers | 6:3-5 | Archives confirm arguments of Jewish elders |
| 10. | 4:21-22 | Order is given to stop the reconstruction of the city | 6:7-10 | Order is given to support the reconstruction of the temple |
| e) | | | 6:11-12 | Sanctions and curse against offenders of the royal decree |
| 11. | 4:23 | Final result: officals obey the royal command. They stop the reconstruction of Jerusalem | 6:13 | Final result: officials obey the royal command |
| | 24 | Reconstruction of temple stays interrupted until the 2nd year of Darius (see 4:5) | 6:14-18 | Reconstruction of temple continues. The temple is completed and dedicated (see 5:5) |
| f) | | | 6:19-22 | Celebration of Passover and of the festival of Unleavened Bread (Hebrew) |

*2.1. The Parallel Elements*

2.1.1. Compositional parallels. The infrequency of the parallel elements and their almost identical sequence forbid consideration of mere coincidence. Rather we find two parallel stories relating to the reconstruction of the temple of Jerusalem in postexilic times.[30] The introductions of both accounts take

---

[30]So already Torrey, *Ezra Studies,* 160f.

pains to point out that both stories refer to the same effort of reconstruction, the one under Zerubbabel and Jeshua.[31] The spokesmen for this enterprise justify their activity as obedience to a command of King Cyrus.[32] Outsiders cause the work on the temple to be stopped or to continue. But in neither case do they feel authorized to settle the matter themselves. They (or other agents of similar position) seek a decision on the highest level. The emperor himself must have the last word. On the other hand provisions are made to avoid an arbitrary royal *ad hoc* decree. The emperor's attention is rather directed to archive materials that will provide enough background information to guide him towards a predictable decision. Enemies of the Jews and the Jews themselves are well acquainted with distinct archive documents that serve their proper purposes. Both the negative and the positive royal decision depend on reading material recommended by subordinates. In both cases the emperor confirms and supports the action taken by the regional authorities who stopped or tolerated the building program.

2.1.2. *Other parallel elements.* In both stories there is a reference to the time of the Israelite monarchy.[33] Both stories return in their final statements to an element at the beginning of each narrative.[34] Both accounts introduce the text of letters to the kings with the rare term "copy of the letter."[35] There is no debate or doubt that the archive materials of the imperial bureaucracy are authentic. This list of parallels could be prolonged.

### 2.2. *The Contrasts within the Parallels*

2.2.1. *Compositional contrasts.* From the beginning to the end both stories show contrasting features. Debates on the legitimacy of the reconstruction of the temple (city) of Jerusalem culminate in royal decrees of prohibition or of support for the enterprise. There are a number of reasons given for such alternative decisions. One has to do with the agents. The participants in the controversy, although implanted long ago by Assyrian kings,[36] are geographically closer[37] than their most remote counterparts in the second story.[38] The

---

[31]Ezra 4:2-3; 5:2 (6:7 LXX). Commentators who separate Ezra 4:1-3 (so Torrey, 184) or Ezra 4:1-5 (so Williamson, 40ff.) from the redactional unit Ezra 4:1-6:22 must ignore this parallel.

[32]Ezra 4:3; 5:13-15.

[33]Ezra 4:20; 5:11.

[34]Ezra 4:24 = 4:5 interrupted reconstruction work; 6:14 = 5:1, 5 reconstruction work, inspired by prophets, continues.

[35]*"parsegen'iggarta',"* only Ezra 4:11 and 5:6 (similar forms: Ezra 7:11; Esther 3:14; 4:8; 8:13); while other references to this correspondence use *"ništevan,"* Ezra 4:7, 18; 5:5, or *"pitgam,"* Ezra 4:17.

[36]Esar-haddon (B.C. 680-669) Ezra 4:2; and Assurbanipal (B.C. 668-632) Ezra 4:10.

[37]See Samaria, 4:10, 17 (though unique in this context).

[38]Tattenai and Shetharboznai (Ezra 5:3, 6; 6:6, 13) are just generally related to the province "Beyond the River" (Transeuphrates).

first have vested interests.[39] They do not inform the emperor about the contention of the Jews that they are obedient to the decree of Cyrus. They rather present their own arguments which are hostile to the Jews. The authors of the letter to Darius, on the other hand, take a rather detached attitude and impartially present the arguments of the elders of the Jews to the emperor. The first group has forcefully interrupted the construction work on the temple before they write to the emperor. The second group permits the continuation of the work, leaving a contrary decision to the emperor. Consequently both parties call attention to different proof texts from royal archives, guiding the emperor toward mutually exclusive decisions. But the negative outcome of the first story had a time limit,[40] while the positive decision has the permanent protection of an imperial decree.[41]

2.2.2. Other contrasting elements. "Enemies of Judah" initiate the action of the first story. The canonical prophets Haggai and Zechariah inaugurate the second. Former great kings of Jerusalem[42] or Israel[43] are presented as politicians with imperial tendencies in one report, while the second refers to one great king as temple builder. The first story accuses the Jews of building up Jerusalem as a military fortress. The second only mentions the reconstruction and equipping of the temple. In the first story people who are not part of the Golah are excluded from the reconstruction of the temple even if they "seek" one and the same God, "Yahweh, the God of Israel."[44] In the second they are included in the Passover celebration if they separate themselves from the nations of the land "to seek Yahweh, the God of Israel."[45] This list could be prolonged again.

### 2.3. Contradictory Elements, or Elements Lacking Parallel or Contrast Function

2.3.1. Compositional contradictory elements. In Ezra 4:6-7 two documents are mentioned,[46] an anonymous accusation (*sitnah*) directed to King Xerxes, and a letter (*ništewan*) to king Artaxerxes from three named[47] and additional unnamed authors. The content of both documents is missing and the names of the authors have no further function. The most probable reason

---

[39]Ezra 4:5.

[40]The time of Darius (4:5) or to his second year (4:24).

[41]Ezra 6:11-12.

[42]"*malkin taqqifin*," Ezra 4:20.

[43]"*melek leyisra'el rab*," Ezra 5:11.

[44]Ezra 4:1-2.

[45]Ezra 6:21.

[46]Elements a-b of the above plot.

[47]There is no other reference to "Bishlam, Mithredath and Tabeel." The numerous speculations relating to their identity (see commentaries) remain uncertain.

for the short reference to these documents would be that they were part of a literary source used by the redactor of this chapter.[48]

All other elements without parallel are found in Ezra 6. In verses 1-2 only after an extensive search is the document found[49] which the elders of the Jews had mentioned in their conversation with governor Tattenai (Ezra 5:9ff). The text of this document is quoted first (Ezra 6:3-5). Only later "quotations" from a response of King Darius confirm the legitimate claims of the Jews, adding updated implementations,[50] which culminate in a new royal decree with severe sanctions for any offender (Ezra 6:10-12). These diverse "documents" are rather forcefully clustered into something similar to a letter.[51] All emphasis rests with these "documents" which are presented in a relatively systematic order, causing the structure of the elements of the two plots to be inverted at some minor points.[52] Again the most probable reason for the inverted order of elements of the plot and for the elements without parallel has to do with the nature of the materials united in this chapter. If the redactor did not dispose of a letter of Darius, his intention to create two parallel plots with the help of rather diverse "documents" will become even more admirable.

The final Hebrew section of Ezra 6:19-22, dealing with the celebration of the first Passah and of the festival of Unleavened Bread, seems to be a creation of the redactor. Its parallel to the Chronicler's account of the Passover of Hezekiah[53] and Josiah[54] in the books of Chronicles can hardly be denied.[55]

---

[48]So most commentators, regardless if they take the Aramaic portions of the book of Ezra to be Jewish writing, almost contemporary with the final redactor (Torrey, *Ezra Studies,* 161; Gunneweg, *Esra,* 86) or a collection of authentic documents (Williamson, "The Composition of Ezra I-VI," *JTS* 34 (1983): 1-30).

[49]The letter of Tattenai seems to point to a concrete royal archive in Babylonia (*bet ginzayya' di malca' tamma' bebabel,* Ezra 5:17). The name is not quite identical with that of the archive at Ecbatana, where the document is found (*bet sifrayya' di ginzayya' mehahatin tamma' bebabel,* Ezra 6:1). This difficulty is often removed through textual criticism.

[50]Ezra 6:6-9.

[51]Recent publications on Aramaic epistolography have not really produced parallels to the structure of Ezra 6:3-12 or 6:6-12. See R. deVaux, "The decrees of Cyrus and Darius on the Rebuilding of the Temple," (1937) in *The Bible and the Ancient Near East,* (London: Darton, Longman & Todd, 1971) 62-96; J. A. Fitzmyer: "Aramaic Epistolography," (1974) in *A Wandering Aramean* (Missoula: Scholars Press, 1979) 183-204 = *Semeia* 22 (1982): 25-57. H. G. M. Williamson is aware of this, surmising that a lost original was in agreement with Aramaic epistolography; "Ezra I-VI," 21.

[52]Elements 8-9 of the above chart.

[53] 2 Chr 30.

[54] 2 Chr 35:1-19.

[55]See H. G. M. Williamson, *JTS* 34 (1983): 29.

Its antithetical function to the introductory verses of Ezra 4:1ff. has been mentioned before[56] and there may be even more antithetical ideas.[57]

2.3.2. Other elements without parallel. The confusing variety of concepts, topics, designations, and terminology is characteristic for the parallel accounts. Some of the exegetical problems resulting from this variety have been mentioned at the beginning of this essay. A detailed study of the text will multiply the problems. Only a few of them can be mentioned in this context. The variety of agents of the two plots is surprising.

The people involved in the construction work are called "Israel,"[58] "Judah and Benjamin,"[59] "the inhabitants of Judah and Jerusalem,"[60] "the people of Judah,"[61] "Jews,"[62] or "exiles."[63] At times all interest is centered on Jerusalem[64] or on "that city."[65] Some titles may point to changing authority structures in Judah in postexilic times. There are references to "heads of the families"[66] and to "elders of the Jews,"[67] as spokesmen for the people, or simply to "those men,"[68] or to the "men at their heads."[69] Individuals like Zerubbabel[70] and Jeshua[71] may be active in the reconstruction of the temple,[72] but in the dialogue with opponents they appear only as members of the "heads of the families,"[73] and their names are never mentioned in the quoted "documents." The prophets Haggai and Zechariah have initiated the restoration of the temple with their prophecies,[74] but they have no function in the con-

---

[56]See above, 2.2.2.

[57]Williamson, ibid, points to the positive function of the priests in Ezra 6:20.

[58]Ezra 4:3; 6:16, 17, 21.

[59]Ezra 4:1.

[60]Ezra 4:6 (Jews in Judah and Jerusalem, Ezra 5:1).

[61]Ezra 4:4.

[62]Ezra 4:12, 23; 5:1, 5; 6:7, 8, 14.

[63]*beney hagolah*: Ezra 4.1; 6:16, 19, 20.

[64]Ezra 4:12, 23.

[65]So only in the letters to and from Artaxerxes: Ezra 4:13, 15, 16, 19, 21.

[66]Ezra 4:2-3 (cf. 1:5; 3:12; 8:1 etc.). See J. P. Weinberg, "Das *beit 'abot* im 6.-4. Jh.v.u.Z." *VT* 23 (1973): 400-14.

[67]Ezra 5:5, 9; 6:7, 8, 14.

[68]Ezra 4:21; 5:4; 6:8.

[69]Ezra 5:10.

[70]Ezra 4:2, 3; 5:2 (6:7 LXX).

[71]Ezra 4:3; 5:2.

[72]Ezra 5:2.

[73]Ezra 4:2, 3.

[74]Ezra 5:1; 6:14.

troversy. Similarly the opponents of the construction program may be named "enemies of Judah and Benjamin"[75] or "people of the land."[76] They may present themselves as offspring of exiles from the time of the Assyrian kings Ezarhaddon[77] or Ashur-banipal.[78] But even as named and prominent authors of letters with impressive titles their individuality seems to disintegrate amidst the anonymity of many named and unnamed co-authors.[79] The "documents," not the individuals, are what is significant.

A similar variety is found in references to God,[80] to the building project proper,[81] and to the many written "documents"[82] of these chapters.

It should not surprise us that a number of words and topics are typical only for one part of the stories. Other words and topics reappear in parallel sections even if they may disturb the context. "Yahweh, the God of Israel," for instance, seems to be original in the introductory verses of Ezra 4:1-3. This name reappears in a more or less complete form in Ezra 6:21f., while the remainder of Ezra 5-6 prefers the designation "Eloha." The construction project is called "*hekal*" (temple) in the introduction, but it is called "*qiryeta'*" and "*šurayya'*" (city and walls) in the remainder of Ezra 4. "*bayta'*" is the technical term for the temple in Ezra 5-6, and also parts of the building

---

[75]Ezra 4:1.

[76]Ezra 4:4.

[77]Ezra 4:2.

[78]Ezra 4:10.

[79]Ezra 4:7-11, 17; 5:3, 6; 6:6, 13.

[80]"Yahweh" (Ezra 4:1, 3; 6:21, 22), "God of Israel" (4:1, 3; 5:1; 6:14, 21, 22), "God of Heaven and earth" (5:11), "God of heaven" (6:10), "the great God" (5:8), "your God" (4:2), "our God" (4:3), "their God" (5:3), "the God who lets his name dwell there" (6:12) or simply "God" (Hebrew: *'elohim* 6:22); Aramaic: *'elah*, *'elaha'* (4:24; 5:2, 13, 14, 15, 16, 17; 6:5, 6, 8, 16, 17, 18).

[81]The temple is called: "*hekal* for Yahweh" (4:1). In all other instances "*hekal*" is used for a royal palace (4:14) or for temples of Babel (5:14, [2x]) or Jerusalem when they are not in construction (5:14, 15; 6:5, [2x], the "house" of God (4:24; 5:2, 8, 13, 14, 15, 16, 17; 6:3, 5, 7, 8, 12, 16, 22), or simply the (that) "house" (5:4, 9, 11, 15; 6:3, 15), the "building" (*binyana'*, 5:4) including the "walls" (*kutlayya'*, 5:8) and woodwork (*'ussarna'* 5:3, 9). For recent literature on *'ussarna'* cf. Williamson, *Ezra, Nehemiah*, 70n3c. The "city" (*qiryeta'*, Ezra 4:10, 12, 13, 15, 16, 18, 21) of Jerusalem and her "walls" (*šurayya'*, Ezra 4:12, 13, 16) are the construction project of the "documents" of Ezra 4.

[82]The letters are referred to as "*sitnah*" ("accusation," Ezra 4:6), "*ništewan*" ("document," 4:7, 18, 23; 5:5) "*iggerah*" ("letter," 4:8, 11; 5:6), "*pitgam*" ("message," 4:17; 5:7 [11]; 6:11); "*sim te 'em*" or "*te 'em*" ("[issued] order," 5:5 [17]) "*gaw*" ("inner part," 5:2; 6:2), or "*paršegen*" ("copy," 4:11, 23; 5:6). A terminological study was done by Paul E. Dion, "Aramaic Words for 'Letter,' " *Semeia* 22 (1982): 77-88. The archive materials or other written sources are called "*sefar dokranayya'*" or "*dikronah*" ("[the book of] records," Ezra 4:15 [2x]; 6:2), "*sim te 'em*" ("issued order," 5:17), simply "*megillah*" ("scroll," 6:2) or by the author's name "*sefar mošeh*" ("The book of Moses," 6:18).

have different names. The mixed terminology for some of the quoted "documents"[83] indicates the redactional intention to give equal importance and weight to all of these documents. The variety and distribution of words and topics reveal redactional activity as well as the existence of originally independent units or "documents."

## 3. THE REDACTION OF EZRA 4-6

### 3.1. The General Purpose and Theological Outlook of the Redactor

Observations on the structure and style of Ezra 4-6 suggest that the present form of these chapters is the result of careful redactional planning. On the other hand there can be hardly any doubt that older "documents" have influenced style and content of the present composition. Leaving aside the complicated question of whether or not these "documents" are historically reliable, their relative independence from the present composition seems to be quite apparent. This can be said not only about the quoted written "documents" but also about some narrative elements.

Ezra 4:1-5 in particular presents features of content and style observably alien to the rest of Ezra 4-6.[84] The position of a rigorous religious party is apparent in this text.[85] The redactor attempts a theological correction of this position[86] by means of his parallel account of two contrasting stories at times utilizing the technique of "repetitive resumption."[87] In Ezra 4:24 he takes up the reference to the interruption of construction work on the temple of Ezra 4:5. By introducing vocabulary from the contrast story of Ezra 5-6, the pivotal function of Ezra 4:24 becomes apparent. The story of rivalries between various groups on matters of the temple and the city of Jerusalem in Ezra 4:1-5 and 4:6-23 does not really find a continuation in the subsequent accounts.

---

[83]"*ništewan*" and "'*iggarta*'" in Ezra 4:11 & 18; "*pitgama*'" and "*ništewan*" in Ezra 4:17 & 23; "'*iggarta*'" and "*pitgama*'" in Ezra 5:6-7.

[84]The contrast to Ezra 6:19-22 has been mentioned before. H. G. M. Williamson observed that "the spirit of . . . 4:1-3 for instance is absolutely foreign to the outlook of the Chronicler." "Ezra I-VI," 27.

[85]E.g. Morton Smith, *Palestine Parties and Politics That Shaped the Old Testament* (New York: Columbia University Press, 1971) 112ff.

[86]The dominant religious and confessional postexilic ecclesiology in opposition to narrow political or national self-definitions has been analyzed recently by Stefan Stiegler, "Die Nachexilische JHWH-Gemeinde in Jerusalem—ein Beitrag zu einer alttestamentlichen Ekklesiologie" (unpublished dissertation, Halle: 1987).

[87]For the use of this technique in Ezra 4:24 cf. Williamson, "Ezra I-VI," 17. The technique was first observed by C. Kuhl, "Die 'Wiederaufnahme'—ein literarkritisches Prinzip?" *ZAW* 66 (1952) 1-11.

Rather, the resumption of the basic terminology of Ezra 4:1-3 (5) at the very
end of the unit in 6:21f. reveals the didactic purpose of the two contrasting
stories. This didactic purpose is responsible for the anachronistic arrangement of documents and events. The reader should learn a lesson: important
and legitimate aims[88] cannot be achieved by means of rigorous arguments or
acts of confrontation which only provoke actions of hostility and frustration.
Adversaries may manipulate the authorities who are mightier and better in-
formed politically. The successful and theologically correct procedure is that
of persuasive theological arguments[89] and of the optimal use of political skill
and know-how[90] as demonstrated by the elders of the Jews. If the Persian king
Darius sponsors sacrifices to the "God of heavens," asking for prayers of
intercession on his own and his sons' behalf,[91] and if he is acquainted with a
theology of Jerusalem as the place "where God lets his name dwell,"[92] then
this must be considered to be a triumph for the God of the Jews. The knowledge and worship of this God cannot be confined to a rigid and narrow Jewish
sect. His cult is open to anybody who accepts the demands of this God.[93]

### 3.2. Redactional Use of Documentary Sourse Material

It is rather unlikely that the redactor should have at his disposal two sets
of original documents from different times with practically identical topic and
structure. If we rule out such miraculous coincidence, the parallel sequence
of events and the contrasting elements of the two plots must be attributed to
the skillful hand of an astute redactor. In this case it is equally unlikely that
the redactor would have changed the original chronological sequence of a
collection of written documents.[94] Even if there is enough compositional and
literary evidence for the use of written source materials,[95] their selection and

---

[88]The theological legitimacy of the temple reconstruction project is underlined through
repeated reference to the God-inspired prophetic initiative (Ezra 5:1f; 6:14).

[89]Particularly the selfpresentation of the elders: ("we are servants of the God of heaven
and earth" [Ezra 5:11]), stresses the apolitical motivation of the enterprise.

[90]The detailed knowledge of the regulations of the edict of Cyrus (Ezra 5:13-15) finds full
confirmation in documents of Persian archives (Ezra 6:3-5). Here the elders draw even with
the knowledge of the adversaries of 4:15, 19f.

[91]The function of this literary device is not affected by the dispute over the historical re-
liability of the decree of Darius. For details of this dispute, cf. R. deVaux, "The Decree of
Cyrus and Darius" (cf. n51), 88ff.

[92]Ezra 6:12; this deuteronomistic formula (cf. Deut 11:21; 14:23f.; 16:2, 6, 11; 26:2) is
unique in the book of Ezra; but cf. Neh 1:9.

[93]Ezra 6:21.

[94]This is a regularly repeated suggestion of those who believe in original documents. So
again Stiegler, "Die JHWH-Gemeinde" (cf. n87), 17.

[95]Cf. below, 2.3.1-2.

their skillful arrangement must be attributed to the redactor alone. However, a detailed study of the variety of forms, historical allusions, and terminology of the source material of Ezra 4-6 is beyond the scope of this paper.

*3.3. Particular Theological Aspects of the Redactor*

3.3.1. A theology of Jerusalem. From the beginning the text is concerned with Jerusalem and its temple. Even King Darius knows the Deuteronomistic idea that God has made his name dwell there.[96] The disturbing combination of "documents" dealing with the fortification of Jerusalem (Ezra 4:[6]12-23) and those dealing with the reconstruction of the temple of Jerusalem (Ezra 4:1-5,24; 5:1-6,18[22]) may point to a development of the Jerusalem-Zion theology which does not distinguish clearly between the sanctity of the city and the sanctity of the temple. Some Zion-Psalms like Psalms 46, 87, and 122 particularly reflect such theology. They may throw some light on the theological position of the redactor of Ezra 4-6.

3.3.2. A theology of scribes. Narrative elements play a minor role in Ezra 4-6. The documents and the knowledge of the documents are the most significant. This knowledge abounds in the text. The redactor presents himself as a learned man. He is acquainted with a fair number of documents. He knows the authors. He is able to quote the texts if it suits his purpose. He knows where documents are archived. He is aware of the fact that literary documents play a decisive role in political decisions. He has learned that those who know how to present the right documents have a tremendous influence upon the decisions of the mighty. He even knows about dangerous documents. Their very existence is a constant threat to Jerusalem.[97] Archives of the Persian court have documents about the imperialistic tendencies of former kings of Jerusalem. Whatever the nature of these documents may be, they need a correction. The Deuteronomistic accounts of the Davidic-Solomonic monarchy[98] unfortunately confirm the dangerous information of the documents. The redactor may even insinuate that the Deuteronomistic history and the dangerous documents are identical. They really need a Chronistic counterpoint, demonstrating that the great kings of Jerusalem were basically concerned with the temple and with religious issues.[99]

This corrective could indeed be part of the *Nachgeschichte* of this text if the books of Chronicles were composed later than Ezra-Nehemiah.[100]

---

[96]Cf. below, 4.1.

[97]Ezra 4:15, 19f.

[98] 1 Sam 16-1 Kgs 11.

[99]On the image of David in the books of Chronicles, cf. Tae-soo Im, *Das Davidbild in den Chronikbüchern* (Bern: Peter Lang, 1985).

[100]Cf. Sara Japhet, "The Supposed Common Authorship of Chronicles and Ezra-Nehemiah Investigated Anew." *VT* 18 (1968): 330-71.

By presenting a series of "historical documents" the redactor opts for an apparently scholarly approach to history. Only what can be documented is historically correct. A history of recent research demonstrates how much modern scholars have been intrigued by his approach. Often these "documents" are taken to be identical with modern historical sources.

However it should not escape the attention of a thorough reader that the very last document mentioned in Ezra 4-6 is the book of Moses.[101] The obedience to this book will safeguard the ritual perfection of the Jerusalem temple worship. "Book history" and "book religion" are parallel aspects of a scribal theology.

3.3.3. In conclusion: The purpose of Reconciliation. Last but not least, the purpose of reconciliation needs special attention. The terminological variety of designations for the people of God in Ezra 4-6[102] points to various Jewish groups who claim the right to be the only legitimate continuation of the people of God, Israel. Particularly the "exiles"[103] from Babylon have claimed special rights under the protection of Persian authorities.[104] The learned redactor of Ezra 4-6 does not demonstrate any preference for a particular Jewish group, opting rather for "all the sons of Israel."[105] He abhors militant sectarianism.

Only a united nation will be able to prevail whenever hostile forces jeopardize its existence. In this respect the redactor agrees with the Chronicler's intention of reconciliation, even if both suggest different alternatives. The Chronicler identifies the total population of Judah with the exiles (2 Chr 36:20ff.), the redactor of Ezra 4-6 with the "sons of Israel." The Chronicler cannot be identified with the redactor of Ezra 4-6. Both use different language and imagery, but their theological positions coincide in many points.

---

[101]Ezra 6:18.

[102]Cf. 2.3.2.

[103]Ezra 4:1; 6:16, 19f.

[104]On the rivalry of particular groups in the book of Jeremiah cf. Karl-Friedrich Pohlmann, *Studien zum Jeremiabuch*, FRLANT 118 (Göttingen: 1978).

[105]Ezra 6:17, 20.

# THE TREATMENT OF
# EARLIER BIBLICAL THEMES
# IN THE BOOK OF DANIEL

REX A. MASON
REGENT'S PARK COLLEGE
OXFORD

There is still little consensus of scholarly opinion on the Book of Daniel. While almost all accept that, in its final form at least, it belongs to the second century B.C., there is little agreement on the relation of the narratives of the first six chapters to the visions of chapters seven to twelve, or on the date of origin of the narratives.[1] Again, a really convincing reason for the change of language from Hebrew to Aramaic between 2:4b-7:28 is still awaited. The question of whether the book is truly "apocalyptic" in nature still receives different answers, while a satisfactory definition of the term "apocalyptic" continues to prove elusive.[2] Another question, not unrelated to the last, still

---

[1]See H. H. Rowley, "The Unity of the Book of Daniel," *Hebrew Union College Anniversary Publication*, Part 1 (Cincinatti: 1952) 233-72; also *The Servant of the Lord & Other Essays* (Oxford: 1965) 247-80, and literature cited there. More recently O. Kaiser, *Introduction to the Old Testament*, trans. John Sturdy (Oxford: 1973) 305-15, and J. J. Collins, *The Apocalyptic Vision of the Book of Daniel* (Harvard: 1977). The issues are discussed in all major commentaries.

[2]Literature on the subject of "Apocalyptic" is extensive and grows apace. Some of the more significant recent works include, P. D. Hanson, ed., *Visionaries & Their Apocalypses* (Philadelphia: London: 1983); *The Dawn of Apocalyptic*, (Philadelphia: 1975); *Daniel, with an Introduction to Apocalyptic Literature, The Forms of the Old Testament Literature*, Vol. XX (Grand Rapids, Michigan: 1984); ed., *Semeia 14: Apocalypse: The Morphology of a Genre* (1979); O. Plöger, *Theocracy & Eschatology*, trans. S. Rudman, (Oxford: 1968); K. Koch, *The Rediscovery of Apocalyptic, Studies in Biblical Theology*, 2nd. Series, trans. M. Kohl (London: 1972); E. W. Nicholson, "Apocalyptic," *Tradition & Interpretation*, G. W. An-

evokes different answers, namely, "What is the source of inspiration of the book?" Is it a "child of prophecy," or does it owe more to Greek and Persian thought?[3] Or, on the other hand, is it a representative of the "Wisdom" literature of the Old Testament?[4] To whom does it refer when it speaks of "the wise"?[5] While there is agreement on the importance of this book as a source of influence on later Jewish apocalyptic, there continue to be very different evaluations of the worth of such literature.[6]

A conclusive solution of so many far-reaching issues lies beyond the scope of this article and the competence of its writer. One aspect of the book, however, has continued to interest him in the course of teaching it to students, namely, the influence of earlier biblical literature and themes on this book and the exegetical use made in it of such material. This is no master-key to unlock every door of critical discussion, but it may prove a small fragment of mosaic helping towards a better grasp of the whole pattern.

*******

The narratives of chapters one to six are often thought individually to have been originally independent of each other, and together of the visions in chapters seven to twelve. The date given in 2:1 conflicts with the three year training period for Daniel and his friends spoken of in 1:5. In chapter two Daniel appears to be unknown to Nebuchadnezzar for, although according to 1:20 he and his friends have been found to be of especial skill in all matters of wisdom, it does not occur to Nebuchadnezzar to consult him concerning his dream of the image. Similarly, in spite of Nebuchadnezzar's honor to Daniel in 2:48, he does not turn to Daniel until 4:8 in regard to the dream of the tree. The pattern of the narratives is not consistent. In chapter two Nebuchadnezzar demands to be told the dream and its interpretation while in chapter four he narrates the dream before asking for its meaning. Again, while only the three friends figure in the story of the fiery furnace in chapter three,

---

derson, ed. (Oxford: 1979); M. A. Knibb, "Prophecy and the Emergence of the Jewish Apocalypses," *Israel's Prophetic Tradition*, R. J. Coggins *et al*. eds. (Cambridge: 1982); C. Rowland, *The Open Heaven. A Study of Apocalyptic in Judaism and Early Christianity* (London: 1982); while two earlier works still remain popular, H. H. Rowley, *The Relevance of Apocalyptic*, 3rd. ed. (London: 1963), and D. S. Russell, *The Method & Message of Jewish Apocalyptic, Old Testament Library* (London: 1964).

[3]See the comprehensive discussion and survey in Koch, *Rediscovery*.

[4]So G. von Rad, *Old Testament Theology*, Vol. II, trans. D. G. M. Stalker (London: 1965) 301ff., and *Wisdom in Israel*. trans. J. Martin (London: 1972) 263ff.

[5]Discussed by O. Plöger, *Theocracy and Eschatology*, 16f.

[6]See the summary of scholarly treatments of the apocalyptic elements in the New Testament, Koch, *Rediscovery*, 57-111.

in other chapters Daniel is the sole Israelite actor. This suggests that in chapter one Daniel may have been introduced into a narrative which once dealt with the three friends in order to give a unity to traditions which originally were separate. It has often been pointed out that the attitude to foreign powers in the narratives is more friendly than that shown in the visions.[7] This has usually been held to indicate that they may have originated in the eastern Diaspora where many Jews had flourished and known happier experiences in their dealings with foreign governments than those experienced by the Jews in Palestine under the Seleucids. A number of accurate historical and social recollections may strengthen this impression.[8] The fact that most of the Persian and Greek loan words in the book occur in the narratives does not really make an earlier date for them impossible, since traditional tales become modified in the course of their transmission, their form and content reflecting changes of vocabulary and circumstances. The editorial process by which they have been brought within the final form of the book seems to have had the two-fold aim of bringing them into an inner unity and of sharpening their relevance and application to the situation in which the Jews found themselves in the second century B.C. under the persecution of Antiochus IV Epiphanes. We cannot always be sure exactly what detail may be assigned to the *Vorlage* (Plöger's phrase) and what has been added in the course of this editorial activity. If, however, this answers to the process which has taken place in the book of Daniel in general terms, we should be able to detect at least three levels at which treatment of earlier biblical themes may have taken place: i) in the narratives themselves; ii) in the visions of chapters seven to twelve; and iii) in the editorial process by which visions and narratives have been combined in the final form of the book.

*******

The narratives concern themselves with just such features of Jewish religion as one would expect to have gained prominence in the time of the Exile and beyond when, without temple and cultic worship, that which distinguished the Jew from his Gentile environment mattered more. Such things as the Jewish dietary laws (chap. 1), the refusal to worship pagan cult objects (chap. 3), and the importance of prayer and other forms of non-cultic worship (chap. 6) were thrown into the foreground. It is strange that no narrative il-

---

[7]Although the attitude to Belshazzar in chap. 5 is hostile, Nebuchadnezzar is spoken of in very positive terms, e.g. in 2:46ff. It is interesting to note that the Septuagint text, especially in chaps. 4-6, shows a tendency to paint a blacker picture.

[8]See, for example, Montgomery, *The Book of Daniel*, *I.C.C.* (Edinburgh: 1927) 89f., 249ff.

lustrates the proper observance of the Sabbath in view of the importance attached to it in the Exile (for example, Jer 17, Gen 1, Isa 56:4, and so forth) and at the time of the Antiochean persecution (I Macc 2:29-38).

The dietary laws assumed in chapter one are to be found in the Holiness Code (for example, Lev 20:24-27) and the Priestly Writing (Lev 3:17; 11:1-47). This does not mean that the idea was first known only in the exilic period. Deuteronomy also legislated concerning clean and unclean foods (14:3-21) and in part this represents a development of an idea already found in the Book of the Covenant, which it quotes (Exod 23:19, see Deut 14:21), while the regulation prohibiting the boiling of a kid in its mother's milk also occurred in the so-called "Ritual Decalogue" (Exod 34:10-26).[9] This particular injunction appears to have constituted a rejection of a Canaanite cultic practice, according to the Ugaritic texts.[10] Since the pig, or wild boar, was considered to be a sacred animal in the Syrian and Phoenician cults,[11] this suggests a strong element of dissociation from foreign cults in the Old Testament dietary laws, although we can certainly not always explain why certain animals were considered unclean.[12] Something of this is seen in Hosea's words that, because of Israel's religious apostasy, the effects of the deliverance from Egypt, by which they had become God's people, would be reversed and they would assume again the cults of foreign gods:

> They shall not remain in the land of the LORD;
> but Ephraim shall return to Egypt,
> and they shall eat unclean food in Assyria. (Hos 9:3)

The *Vorlage* of chapter one in the book of Daniel refuses to accept this as inevitable. The exiles, although in a foreign land, need not know this judgement. Even there they could remain faithful to Yahweh's law and, if they did, he would keep and prosper them. Thus, not only does this narrative show a more positive attitude towards foreign powers, but towards the experience of Exile itself. Far from being just the negative judgement of Yahweh, the Exile can prove a valid experience of his power and grace. It echoes the spirit of Jeremiah's letter to the exiles (Jer 29:4-28).[13]

---

[9]See H. H. Rowley, "Moses & The Decalogue," *BJRL* 34 (1951): 81-118 = *Men of God* (London: 1963) 1-36 for a discussion of the "Ritual Decalogue" of Exod 34. For more recent evaluations see E. W. Nicholson, *God and His People* (Oxford: 1986) 134-50.

[10]Text 52, 1.14. See B. S. Childs, *Exodus,* OTL (London: 1974) 485f.

[11]M. Noth, *The Laws in the Pentateuch & Other Essays,* trans. D. R. Ap-Thomas (London: 1966) 57f.

[12]See also J. Milgrom, "The Biblical Dietary Laws as an Ethical System," *Interpretation* 16 (1973): 288-301.

[13]Almost certainly, Jer 29 must be seen as belonging to the Deuteronomistic sections of the book of Jeremiah, a fact which makes it of immediate relevance to the exiles in Babylon. See E. W. Nicholson, *Preaching to the Exiles* (Oxford: 1970) 97-100.

Here a word may be included on the strong "Wisdom" elements in the vocabulary of this chapter, especially in verses 4, 17 and 20. With its themes of the prospering of God's people if they remain obedient to his will, even in an alien environment, it strongly recalls the Joseph "Novelle" with its strong "Wisdom" associations (Gen 37:39-48). Nevertheless, it seems difficult to follow von Rad in finding the Wisdom literature of the Old Testament as one of the main sources of inspiration for the book[14] since it is concerned broadly with matters of cult in the narratives and eschatology in the visions, neither being a prime concern of the Wisdom writers. It is more likely to be explained as a deliberate contrast to the great emphasis on Wisdom in Babylon and to have been influenced by the prophetic insistence that true wisdom comes from Yahweh alone.[15] This would explain the repeated emphasis in the narratives, not on the wisdom of Daniel, but upon that true wisdom of which Yahweh alone is the source.[16]

In chapter six Daniel is shown as a model of piety whose practice it was to pray three times a day (v 10). There is strikingly little reference to prayer as a non-cultic, private religious activity in the earlier part of the Old Testament (which is not at all the same as saying that it was unknown). Instances of it are recorded of both Ezra (9:7-15) and Nehemiah (1:5-11) and it characterizes Daniel himself in the visions (9:3-19). In each of these instances the note of penitence is stressed. Elsewhere it represents a note of almost helpless dependence on Yahweh, as with Hezekiah (Isa 38:2) or Solomon dedicating the temple (I Kgs 8:23-53), a Deuteronomistic passage which specifically mentions the practice of those in Exile praying *towards* Jerusalem (I Kgs 8:35; see Dan 6:10). This note of dependence is heard most strongly in the Psalms of lament, a Psalm such as Psalm 55 being of special interest, since it mentions the practice of praying three times a day (v 18/17). This occurs at the moment of transition from despair to confidence.[17]

With such general Old Testament background, therefore, may we see in the *Vorlage* of the narrative of chapter six a call to the exiles to show Daniel's spirit of faithful prayer in which penitence towards Yahweh and faith in him find their clearest expression?

It is possible that a similar note is evoked by the use of the "pit" of lions in the story. Just as God delivered the Psalmist from the "Pit" (Pss 40:3/2; 57:5,7/4,6), so God will deliver his people in Exile. Indeed, with the descrip-

---

[14]See n4.

[15]E.g. Isa 5:21, 10:13f., 28:24-29, Jer 9:11f./12f., etc.

[16]E.g., 1:17,21, 2:21-23, 4:18, 5:13.

[17]See S. Mowinckel, *The Psalms in Israel's Worship*, trans. D. R. Ap-Thomas (Oxford: 1962) 1:217f., and H. Gunkel, Begrich, *Einleitung in die Psalmen* HAT (1933) 6: 3.

tion of the Psalmist's enemies in the second of these Psalms as "lions," perhaps we can see, with a number of commentators, a tale in chapter six expounding the truth of Ps 57:5,7/4,6).[18] Such language of the "Pit" could apparently be used in a general figurative sense of God's judgement (see Ezekiel's threat to Tyre of future subjugation by Nebuchadnezzar, Ezek 26:20). It seems to have furnished also a salvation theme of God's deliverance, embodied in specific instances such as those of Joseph being delivered from the "Pit" (Gen 37:24ff.) and Jeremiah (Jer 38:6ff.). So again we appear to have a narrative making use of imagery to show that even in Exile trust in Yahweh would bring a delivering experience of God's presence. Chapter six, like chapter one, thus shows a very positive attitude towards the experience of the Exile.

In the story of the fiery furnace the three friends suffer for their fidelity to Yahweh, not for their sin. Yet it is not difficult to see that the furnace could be pictured as itself a test of fidelity and a divinely-appointed means of demonstrating his power to deliver his people from the most extreme situations. The Deuteronomic literature more than once pictures the Egyptian bondage, and release from it, as a furnace from which Yahweh rescued his people.[19] The picture is used by Ezekiel of the Babylonian siege of Jerusalem in characteristically radical fashion.[20] For him there is no question of the refining process producing a valuable residue, for Israel is totally corrupt. Just as negative a picture of the process occurs in Jeremiah 6:27-30.[21] Second Isaiah also employs the image to speak of the Babylonian exile.[22] Unfortunately, uncertainty about the text here makes for difficulty of interpretation. The MT has:

I have smelted you, but not with silver,
I have chosen you in the furnace of affliction. (Isa 48:10).

RSV emends the preposition *beth* to *kaph*, giving not "with silver" but "like silver," although this still yields little sense. Some take it as the *beth pretiae*, "I smelted you, but not for the price of silver," that is, "I gained no profit from it."[23] This would mean that Israel was wholly corrupt and God's action in choosing her was one of sheer grace.[24] This brings Second Isaiah's thought

---

[18]Bentzen, *Daniel* HAT (1952) 55.

[19]Deut 4:20, I Kgs 8:51, Jer 11:4.

[20]Ezek 22:17-22.

[21]It is unlikely, therefore, that Ezek 22:22 represents a secondary attempt to interpret the process positively. Wevers' *Ezekiel, New Century Bible*, (London: 1969) 175.

[22]Isa 48:10.

[23]See Gesenius-Kautsch, *Hebrew Grammar*, 2nd. ed. (Oxford: 1910) §119.

[24]So C. R. North, *The Second Isaiah* (Oxford: 1964) 178f.

close to that of Ezekiel. But even the *bᵉḥartîkā*, "I chose you," has an interesting variant in 1QIsaᵃ which gives the translation," I tried you (*bᵉḥantîkā*) in the furnace of affliction and this gives a better parallelism. All one can say is that the Exile is spoken of as a furnace of affliction and testing. By echoing the Deuteronomic description of the Egyptian bondage in such terms, this prophet offers yet another parallel between the Exodus and the approaching release from Babylon. Yahweh is about to deliver them from this also "for his name's sake" (v 11), a stress also found in Ezekiel. But this "name" motif also finds great emphasis in the book of Daniel, both here in chapter three and in the other narratives. Even heathen potentates come to acknowledge Yahweh's great "name," that is, his power as a deliverer (3:28-30, see 2:47-49, 4:34f; 6:25-27).

The appropriateness of this story as originally related to the situation of the Jews in Exile can readily be seen in the obvious danger of worship of cult objects other than Yahweh at such a time. That this danger was real can be seen from Second Isaiah's address to the kind of laments which must often have been heard among the exiled community complaining that Yahweh had proved unable to deliver them (see 40:27-31) or had wearied of them, together with the fierce denunciation of the cults of the Babylonian deities which he makes (for example, 46:1-7). Of course the introduction into the temple of the cult of Olympian Zeus by Antiochus IV would have sharpened the application of such words to the time of the second century B.C. but behind this we can see in the original *Vorlage* another popular exposition of prophetic themes, especially of themes emanating from the prophets of the Babylonian exile.

In similar manner Daniel 4 presents several points of interest. A number of commentators have suggested that Nebuchadnezzar's dream of a great tree is based on earlier motifs in Ezekiel.[25] The closest resemblance is to Ezek 31:3-14 where the same simile is applied in similar language to Pharaoh of Egypt. Perhaps the basis for this, as well as a wide variety of forms of the motif, is an ancient myth of the cosmic tree.[26] To this poem in the book of Ezekiel have been added two different interpretative oracles (vv 10-14 and 15-18), both of which predict the tree's downfall, a downfall which illustrates the theme of judgement against human "hubris." Such a familiar theme also finds echo in Ps 37:36f./35f.

> I have seen a wicked man overbearing,
> and towering like a cedar of Lebanon.

---

[25]So N. Porteous, *Daniel*, OTL (London: 1965) 65f., Plöger, *Das Buch Daniel*, KAT (1965) 74.

[26]Bentzen, *Daniel*, 41f.

Again I passed by, and, lo, he was no more;
though I sought him, he could not be found.

The same theme appears also, perhaps in a context of judgement against Judah, in Ezek 17:1-10. This receives a first explanation in verses 11-21, relating it in detail to Zedekiah, and a second in verses 22-24, a later oracle of
messianic promise which culminates in the knowledge by all the trees that
"Yahweh brings low the high tree and makes high the low tree." Probably
this was the original burden of the narrative in Daniel 4 but the image of a
stump of a tree which has been cut down is abandoned in verse 15, or reduced
to absurdity by a secondary theme. This theme is the mental illness of Nebuchadnezzar who will be driven out into the countryside to live with the
beasts, while his human mind is changed to that of a beast for "seven times."
Yet perhaps this secondary theme itself echoes another prophetic tradition.
In Jer 27:1-7, at the beginning of a three chapter section concerned with Jeremiah's conflict with the false prophets, Jeremiah is directed to make yoke
bars and place them on his neck. This is to counter ambassadors of neigh-
bouring countries who have come to the Jewish community in the time of
Zedekiah[27] perhaps with a view to joint action against the Babylonians. Jeremiah insists that Nebuchadnezzar rules by divine appointment:

It is I who by my great power and outstretched arm have made the earth with
the men and animals that are on the earth, and I give it to whomever it seems
right to me. (v 25)

This is echoed closely in Dan 4:17:

the Most High rules the kingdom of men, and gives it to whom he will, and
sets over it the lowliest of men.

Jeremiah continues:

Now I have given all these lands into the hand of Nebuchadnezzar, the king
of Babylon, my servant, and I have given him also the beasts of the field to
serve him. All the nations shall serve him and his son and his grandson, until
the time of his own land comes; then many nations and great kings shall make
him their slave.

This opening section of Jeremiah 27-29 is usually assigned to the Deuteronomistic tradition,[28] with its own special interest in the theme of true and false
prophecy. Perhaps based on an incident and oracle in Jeremiah's own life, it
would have gained relevance as a word addressed to the exiles. They should
settle down under a rule which is of God's appointment and leave to him its

---

[27]The reference to Jehoiakim in v 1 must be wrong, as the mention of Zedekiah in vv 3,12
makes clear.

[28]See E. W. Nicholson, *Preaching*, 93ff.

final overthrow rather than taking action of their own as the false prophets were calling them to do. The addition to the dream of the tree in Daniel 4 introduces a motif which might well be seen as a promise that the final over-throw is about to be fulfilled. For now, Nebuchadnezzar, to whom had been given the possession and service of men and animals, is to be "driven from among men" (v 32) and his lot is to be "with the beasts in the grass of the earth" (v 15) while his mind is changed from that of a man to a beast (v 16). At what stage this addition could have been made to the original tree narrative it is impossible to say, but its particular relevance to Antiochus IV, nick-named "Epimanes' " "Madman," is clear. As the Babylonian subjugation passed according to the earlier prophetic word, so will that under which they now labor.

The story of Belshazzar's feasting and the divine retribution which falls on him, narrated in chapter five, is closely related to chapter four. Reference back to the earlier story is made in verses 18-21, although it is to that section of the chapter dealing with Nebuchadnezzar's madness which, we saw reason to believe, was a secondary expansion of the dream of the tree. Again in chapter five Belshazzar is spoken of as Nebuchadnezzar's "son," which not only links him with the previous incident but provides an interesting, al-though not exact, echo of Jeremiah 27 which says that the time of Nebu-chadnezzar's land would come after his son and grandson. Yet there are striking differences. Belshazzar is seen in a much more hostile light than the foreign kings in the other stories who, when they see Israel's God acting, do make some sort of response. Belshazzar does not, although he is said to have honored Daniel for his interpretation of the writing. Again, the emphasis here is not so much on "hubris" as on sacrilege and idolatry, on the unspeakable abomination of desecrating the sacred vessels of the Jerusalem temple. While this may well express a certain proud defiance, it might also suggest that this story reflects a later stage than the others when, already, the desecration of that which was sacred to Yahweh had taken place and the attitude of the pious to their foreign overlords and/or their own apostate leaders was hardening. This would also explain reference to chapter four in its later, expanded form.

The mention of the fingers which wrote the words of judgement could have recalled to Jews that it was the finger of God which, in the tradition, had been said to inscribe the commandments.[29] Those very commandments called for the exclusive worship of Yahweh alone. It was to the same divine "fin-ger" that the Egyptian magicians had ascribed the confusion brought about by the plagues which had been seen as judgement for disobedience to the di-vine word.[30] Reference to the sacred temple treasures might well have stirred

---

[29]Exod 31:18, Deut 9:10.

[30]Exod 8:19.

in the hearers' minds the tradition passed down by the Chronicler (or that part
of the "Chronicler tradition" responsible for II Chronicles 36 and Ezra 1:7)
that these very vessels had been restored to their rightful use after the Exile,
in fulfilment of the promise of Second Isaiah:

> Go out from the midst of her, purifying yourselves, you who bear the ves-
> sels of the LORD. (Isa 52:11)

As we shall see, the Chronicler's reference to these vessels is used by the final
compiler of the book of Daniel for a rather different theological purpose. But
here in the narrative it is stressed that those who despise the name of Yahweh
and desecrate the sacred cult vessels are sure to be thwarted. In the end, as
the exilic prophets had confidently predicted, Yahweh will act to vindicate
the honor of his name.

Chapters two and seven present a wide range of problems of interpretation and also of their relation to each other and to the rest of the book. It was
the similarity between these chapters, together with the close relation of
chapter seven to the visions of the later chapters, which convinced Rowley
of the essential unity of the book.[31] In a running battle with Ginsberg on this
issue,[32] a battle marked by the explosive sound of footnotes of increasing
acerbity on both sides, he contested Ginsberg's view that chapter seven had
originally stood as an apocalypse to be dated before the desecration of the
temple in B. C. 167. To this had been added, Ginsberg believed, references
to the "Little Horn" in verses 8,11a, 20b-22, and 25, bringing it into line
with the later visions. M. Noth adopted a very similar position.[33] Rowley's
objection to this view was closely followed by Porteous who argued that the
theory failed

> to produce a situation of sufficient urgency to account for the conviction that
> the supernatural destruction of the fourth kingdom was imminent. Without
> the symbolic reference to Antiochus Epiphanes . . . who was challenging
> the authority of God as none of his predecessors had done, the chapter loses
> its point.[34]

What appears more likely is that it was chapter two which received additions
to bring it into line with chapter seven and the message of the visions of chapters eight to twelve. Chapter seven, by form and content, belongs with the

---

[31]"The Unity of the Book of Daniel," *Servant*, 262ff.

[32]Ginsberg, *Studies in Daniel* (New York: 1948); *JBL* 68 (1949): 402-07; *VT* 4 (1954):
245-75.

[33]*TSK* 98/99 (1926): 143-63.

[34]*Daniel*, 97.

second half of the book. It is a vision of Daniel himself and shows much the same time scheme and eschatology of the later visions. On the other hand it is much easier to see behind chapter two a story in the same style and on the same theme as the other narratives of chapters one to six. This is also a dream of Nebuchadnezzar which Daniel is enabled both to recount and to interpret. The dream of the great image is very similar to that of the tall tree in chapter four. Both could equally well serve to symbolize the greatness of Nebuchad-nezzar's empire. Its description in 2:37f. again closely resembles the descrip-tion of Nebuchadnezzar's God-given rule in Jer 27:5. Yet, the original narrative probably said, that kingdom rested on very insecure foundations. It was doomed, like every human empire before it and after it, to an eventual downfall brought about by God through gradual decline and fatal inner di-visions. The vaunting ambition they represent becomes ripe for judgement. That is exactly a major theme of the other narratives.

Yet, by his attempt to make historical identification of the types of metal, perhaps originally designed to show the decline of the empire, the author has related this story to a four world empire view of history culminating in a final irruption of the kingdom of God, thus bringing it into line with the eschatol-ogy of chapter seven and the later visions. But the material did not lend itself to a reference to the "little Horn," and he is left with the awkward fact that all four empires are thus pictured as being brought down at the same time. In chapter seven, however, the natural explanation of verses 3-7 is that it is the last beast which sprouted the horn which is specifically said to be destroyed. It is true that the logic of the chapter to that point is broken by the obscure reference in verse 12 to the fact that, although the dominion of the other beasts was taken away, their lives were prolonged "for a season and a time." This itself might be an attempt to harmonize the vision with that of chapter two or, as Heaton argued, to explain the prophetic tradition that the heathen nations would serve the people of God (see v 27).[35] Chapter two, then, may well have expressed originally the familiar prophetic theme that God would bring down all that was high and lofty, as in Isa 2:6-19, whose refrain runs:

> And the haughtiness of man shall be humbled
> and the pride of man shall be brought low,
> and the LORD alone will be exalted on that day.

Perhaps the stone which brings all down, but then itself fills the earth, be-coming a great mountain, recalls another prophetic theme, that of the stone which Yahweh lays in Zion (Isa 28:10) which is to become the mountain higher than all others, the place of Yahweh's world rule and the centre of pilgrimage for all the nations (Isa 2:2-4 = Mic 4:1-3).

---

[35]*Daniel, Torch Bible Commentary* (London: 1956) 181.

Thus the narratives of chapters one to six, even in their earlier form and use, seem to have served a number of theological purposes. They assured the Jews of the Diaspora of the sovereignty of Yahweh, far above all objects of pagan worship. He was able to keep and prosper his people in the most adverse circumstances. He alone could impart true wisdom by which to see the real significance of the mysterious events through which their faith was being tested. So viewed, even the apparently disastrous and meaningless event of the Exile was a means of testing and refining them and, by his deliverance of them from it, other nations would be forced to acknowledge that Yahweh truly was God. Therefore the stories called for continued obedience to the Torah and fidelity through all testing. Yet, unless we are to place all these narratives literally in the period of the Babylonian Exile,[36] we must assume that already that Exile had come to have symbolic significance. It must have been seen as something of a "paradigm" experience, symbolizing the continuing dispersion, sufferings and adversities of the people of God. The theological reasons for that Exile, the experience of the people throughout it and the hope of final deliverance from it voiced by the exilic prophets, all were seen to apply with a continuing relevance to the later fortunes of Jews at home and abroad. It is this theme which, it seems, the author of the book has taken up and applied to the suffering in the time of Antiochus IV. Here he found a means by which to bind together narratives and visions.

*******

The account of Nebuchadnezzar's siege and conquest of Jerusalem in the third year of Jehoiakim's reign (1:1ff.)[37] is of interest. It is often argued that this otherwise unknown historical event is based on the Chronicler's tradition of an attack against, and capture of, Jehoiakim by Nebuchadnezzar (II Chr 36:5-8). This is strengthened by the echo of his statement that Nebuchadnezzar took with him "*some* of the vessels of the house of the LORD" (II Chr 36:7; see Dan 1:2).[38] The Chronicler wants to stress the note of continuity, found in the fact that the *identical* vessels were used in the worship of the second temple as had been used in the first.[39] In the same chapter the Chron-

---

[36]As J. J. Collins does, *The Apocalyptic Vision.* 55.

[37]An historical error, usually taken as being based on II Kgs 24:1 and II Chr 36:5-8.

[38]The text in Dan 1:2 reads *miqṣāh kᵉlê bêt-hā'*. The Chronicler uses the more classical Hebrew construction with *min* to indicate "some of. . . ."

[39]So R. J. Coggins, *The First and Second Books of the Chronicles,* CBC, 304f. The whole theme of "Continuity" is examined by P. R. Ackroyd, "The Temple Vessels: A Continuity Theme," *Studies in the Religion of Ancient Israel,* VTSup 23, (1972): 166-81, reprinted in *Studies in the Religious Tradition of the Old Testament* (London: 1987) 46-60.

icler has to explain the break of continuity caused by the Exile. He does so by allusion to the "seventy years" exile of Jeremiah,[40] in which he finds theological purpose for the Exile. The land had to enjoy its sabbaths (II Chr 36:21), in other words to lie fallow and be cleansed of the sins of its former inhabitants (see Lev 2:6; 26:34ff.). The Chronicler had already shown (v 14) that the priests and people had, by their sin, "polluted" the sacred temple in Jerusalem. For this there was "no remedy" (vv 15f.). For him, therefore, the Exile was, in Myers words, "a purifying process carried out in line with the law . . . and the prophets."[41]

The writer of the book of Daniel also calls on Jeremiah's "seventy years of exile" prophecy. It is revealed to Daniel that this really meant "seventy weeks of years" (9:2, 24ff.), an interesting echo of the Chronicler's idea of "sabbath years." He says that the purpose of this period was "to finish the transgression, to put an end to sin and to atone for iniquity" (v 24). Thus he sees a similar cleansing process and purpose in the Exile which concerns both "people" and "holy city" (v 24).[42] But to which period is the writer now referring? Not, as the Chronicler did, to the literal period of the historical Babylonian Exile, but to the whole period from the fall of Jerusalem to *the present events of his own time.* In this seventy weeks of years time scale, the literal return from exile was only an incident, a stage-post in an ongoing process, dealt with in one verse (v 25) and otherwise never referred to in the book. Thus the writer takes both Jeremiah's prophecy concerning the Exile and the Chronicler's theological interpretation of its purpose and significance, and related that to the whole period from that time until his own day, a period which he sees as what we might term a continuing "Babylonish captivity of the people of God." [43] Thus he takes up in the editing of the narratives and the visions, a suggestion we have seen to be implicit in the original narratives themselves.

Perhaps this is why there are such clear allusions in the visions to prophecies which relate to the time of the Exile. Their promises of deliverance from that Exile are taken up in the book of Daniel and applied to the coming deliverance from the present time of distress. One may note the striking parallels in the form and presentation of the visions to those of Ezekiel and, to some

---

[40]Jer 25:11, 29:10.

[41]*II Chronicles, Anchor Bible* (New York: 1965) 223.

[42]Commentators disagree as to whether "a most holy" refers to the temple or to a person. Among commentators who see here a reference to the temple are Montgomery, Plöger, Heaton, Driver, Porteous. LaCocque follows the Vulgate, Peshitta, Hippolytus and traditional Jewish exegesis in seeing it as referring to a person, symbolizing the "saints of the Most High," Israel viewed as "a kingdom of Priests." *The Book of Daniel* (London: 1979) 193f.

[43]A point made by P. R. Ackroyd, *Exile and Restoration* (London: 1968) 242f.

extent, of Zechariah. Daniel sees "visions by night" (7:2) as did Zechariah, a form whose significance the writer has discussed elsewhere.[44] The account of the vision of Gabriel in 8:15ff. closely echoes Ezekiel's call vision, described in Ezekiel 1. This too is by the banks of a river; like Ezekiel, Daniel falls upon his face and is addressed by the term "son of man." The same vision of Ezekiel seems also to be echoed in Dan 10:4ff. Ezekiel's vision assured him of God's presence with him in exile. Although he was commissioned to bring a message of judgement to those who refused to listen, he was also to point to a hope of renewal and deliverance by God's grace beyond the disaster of the fall of Jerusalem. By reminding his readers of this the writer of the book of Daniel assures them that Ezekiel's hope is a present word of God to them. Similarly, he alludes to other exilic prophecies which promised hope beyond the Exile.

We have seen how Jeremiah's prophecy is reinterpreted in chapter nine. Perhaps even more remarkable is the apparent echo of Second Isaiah's "Servant" passages in the writer's description of the "wise" in 11:33-35 and 12:2-4. There have been many ways of understanding his use of this term. G. von Rad found evidence here to support his view that Apocalyptic literature derived from the Wisdom circles.[45] Plöger believed it referred to those who saw the truly eschatological significance in contemporary events, as opposed to those for whom it appeared to be just one more severe crisis in their nation's history.[46] The very great emphasis on Torah in the book of Daniel would suggest that we have a much closer approchement between the so-called "theocratic" and "apocalyptic" circles than Plöger allowed. Hence, perhaps, we should see in the reference to the "wise" those who saw the real values to hold on to during the time of crisis and who had confidence in God's ability to bring final victory.

In any event, what is said of their role closely echoes the role of the Servant as Second Isaiah saw it. The (Heb. *maśkîlê 'ām*) "wise of the people" shall give understanding "to the many" (Heb. *yabînû lārabbîm*) "and [the two things are made parallel by the conjunction] they shall fall by the sword, by captivity and by plunder, for some days." In Isa 53:11 it is said of the Servant, "by his knowledge shall my righteous servant[47] make the many to be accounted righteous [*lārabbîm . . . yaṣdîq*]." Again, in Dan 12:3, the wise

---

[44]*The Books of Haggai, Zechariah and Malachi*, CBC (1977) 29ff.

[45]See n4, and also C. Rowlands, *The Open Heaven*, who, in insisting that the essential feature of the form of the genre Apocalyptic is a directly mediated revelation of knowledge to a special individual, opens the way to viewing it agan as a kind of "Gnosis" or "Wisdom."

[46]*Theocracy & Eschatology*, 16f.

[47]It may be that the *ṣaddîq* of the strange construction *ṣaddâ 'abdî* should be omitted, but it is defended by North, *The Second Isaiah*, 232f.

are described as those who "make the many to be accounted righteous [*maṣ-dîqê hārabbîm*]." If there is direct allusion to the Servant passages here[48] it shows how the idea of the Servant could be, and was, reinterpreted in later situations. It is even possible that the promise contained in the fourth Servant song—

> Kings shall shut their mouths because of him;
> for that which has not been told them they shall
>                          see,
> and that which they have not heard they shall
>                          understand. (Isa 52:15)

is seen by the final author to find its fulfilment in the narratives in which, by the faithful and obedient suffering of Daniel and his friends, foreign kings come to acknowledge the supremacy of Israel's God and his wisdom (3:28-30; 4:37; 6:25-27). Could this also be why so much repeated emphasis is placed on the physical and mental suffering endured by Daniel for being the bearer of the revelation of the heavenly visions (for example, 8:18,27; 10:8-10, 15)?

This seems to show that this writer saw the suffering of the faithful to have a vicarious role. Such a view counsels caution before consigning the book of Daniel to a bundle neatly labelled "apocalyptic," one of whose characteristics is said to be that it sees no action of God in present world history. Like so many neat divisions found between "apocalyptic" and "prophecy" this turns out to be illusory on closer examination.[49] The writer of the book of Daniel does see a purpose of God being worked out in the present events of this world's history.

Perhaps we can go farther. This second reference to the "wise" in 12:3 occurs in a context of the least ambiguous reference to the resurrection of (at least some of) the dead in the Old Testament. Is it possible that this hope also was inspired by the concluding section of Isaiah 53? The later verses of that chapter are notoriously difficult to interpret and their text is in uncertain state. Yet the suggestion is that the Servant will be permitted to see that it was all "worth it," whether or not it is implied that will be in his present lifetime or after his death. Yet this faith should not lead us to leap to exaggerated claims for the so-called "other-worldliness" of the book's eschatology. The writer is simply saying that the faithful who have missed the final victory of God will be raised to experience it and those wicked who have escaped judgment

---

[48]No one is more emphatic about this than M. Fishbane, *Biblical Interpretation in Ancient Israel* (Oxford: 1985) 493. "Quite certainly, the author of Dan 11-12 wished to stress that his group was heir to the mantle of the suffering servant of YHWH."

[49]See J. Barton, *Oracles of God. Perceptions of Ancient Prophecy in Israel after the Exile* (London: 1986) esp. 200-02.

by a conveniently timed death will also be brought back to suffer punishment, not necessarily setting the whole salvation scene in "another" world.

Once more, then, the use of such themes of exilic prophecy confirms the impression that the writer saw the present distress in terms of an extended exile whose purpose was to cleanse and prepare a people for the final victory of God. It is this view—that the author saw his own time as bound theologically to the historic Babylonian Exile, and the earlier promises of God's deliverance from it as about to be fulfilled—which offers us another possible reason for his setting all his prophecy in the time of that Exile and placing it in the mouth of one of the legendary heroes of that period (see Ezek 14:14,20; 28:3). In stating this so clearly he has skilfully expounded a basic view of the Exile already present in the narratives which he took over.

We may ask finally what exactly was envisioned as happening at the time of the final victory? The precise nature of it remains as vague as it is in the exilic prophecy itself. The time scales and historical details of the vision in chapters ten to twelve point to an expectation of the death of Antiochus, the cleansing of the temple and the resumption of purified worship as the climax of the whole process.[50] What exactly is to follow? Dan 9:24 speaks first of the negative side to the process, "ending rebellion," "sealing up sin" and "atoning for iniquity," a purpose we have seen to be in harmony with the Chronicler's view of the purpose of the Babylonian Exile. The positive aim is to "bring in everlasting righteousness" or, if ṣedeq is used with the force it has in Second Isaiah, a permanent "victory" of God's purposes; the "sealing of the vision and the prophecy," that is, the fulfilment of all to which the prophets pointed forward, and "the anointing a most holy," presumably a reference to the resumption of the temple cult.[51] This seems to be more akin to a vision of the renewal of the kind of theocracy envisioned by the Priestly writers and the Chronicler than the vision of that radical renewal of heaven and earth which is supposed to be the hallmark which distinguishes apocalyptic from prophecy. We must always allow for the possibility that ancient writers saw no absolute distinction between the heavenly temple and its earthly counterpart or, indeed, between the heavenly realm and the terrestial one.[52] But is this any more true of so-called "apocalyptic" than it is of prophecy generally? Perhaps the enigmatic vision of chapter seven may throw some light on the matter.

The chapter begins with a vision of a "great sea" stirred up by the "four winds of heaven." There seems to be some reminder of Genesis 1. In place

---

[50]It is not clear on what grounds J. J. Collins can say, "No interest is expressed in the ongoing worship in the temple." *The Apocalyptic Vision,* 165.

[51]See n42.

[52]As Collins stresses, *The Apocalyptic Vision,* 165.

of the "great wind" or "spirit of God" which comes upon the ocean there, the "four winds of heaven" remind us of the visions of Zechariah (Zech 2:10/ 6; 6:5). In Zechariah, these not only indicate the four corners of the earth, but occur in a context, first, of a call to exiled Jews to return to Zion in the light of God's saving activity and, secondly, of the chariots which come to God from all parts of the earth to report that all is now at rest, for now his writ runs everywhere.[53] No really satisfactory explanation for the symbolism of the four animals has been found. There is biblical warrant for the picture of Nebuchadnezzar as a lion (Jer 49:19, and so forth), but no such specific texts link the Medes with bears or the Persians with leopards (the fourth beast remains un-named perhaps to indicate that it is incomparable in its ferocity). Such general prophetic passages as Hos 13:7f. might well furnish the symbolism, however:

> So I will be to them like a lion,
> like a leopard I will lurk beside the way.
> I will fall upon them like a bear robbed of her
> cubs . . . .

Perhaps the proverbial speed of Cyrus's conquests (Isa 41:3) might explain the identification of him with a leopard. Attempts to press examples of early art or to find here allusions to signs of the Zodiac seem more hazardous and improbable. The beasts represent the kingdoms of the world[54] and, at its simplest, it seems best to see the representative of the kingdom of God, depicted as "one like a son of man," that is, "a man," as being in contrast to these other kingdoms. Even the idea of four stages of world history leading to the kingdom of God need not necessarily imply dependence on Zoroastrian conceptions, for the Priestly Writing had already introduced a program of world history leading from Adam to Noah, Noah to Abraham, Abraham to Moses, culminating in the establishment of the theocratic community on Mount Sinai.

The background of chapter seven is the kingly rule of God, threatened by the forces of chaos, but finally established as all the world comes under his rule, all rebellion is ended and order throughout the world is thus established for his people for all time. We do not need to trace too direct a line from this back to the Babylonian creation myth or, with Bentzen,[55] to dependence on a supposed pre-exilic New Year Enthronement Festival. The general ideas of Daniel 7 are all present in the so-called "Enthronement Psalms," whatever their original cultic setting, and these have clearly exercised strong influence

---

[53]For a discussion of the exegetical problems of Zech 6:1-8, see P. R. Ackroyd *Exile & Restoration*, 182f., and R. A. Mason, *Haggai, Zechariah and Malachi*, 59ff.

[54]Cf. the role of "animals" as symbols of enemies in some Psalms, e.g. Ps 22.

[55]*Daniel*, 61.

on the language and imagery of Second Isaiah.[56] The same idea of conflict is found in a "royal" Psalm like Psalm 2 in which the "kings of the earth" set themselves against the rule of God exercised through his "anointed one." Even the thought of Psalm 8, with its stress on the special role given to man by God to mediate his rule over the earth and its animal kingdom, suggests that there are plenty of biblical motifs behind the thought and imagery of Daniel 7. It seems safer to look to these than to insist on dubious cultic and mythological links for which the text itself provides at best ambiguous evidence.

The description of God as the "Ancient of Days" is unique in the Old Testament. It has been argued that it reflects the description of El in the Ugaritic literature as the "Father of Years" and, by analogy, that the description of "one like the son of man" coming "with the clouds of heaven" echoes the description of Baal as the "Rider of the Clouds," the whole background therefore being one of Canaanite mythology.[57] Why the phrase "Father of Years" should become "Ancient of Days" is not obvious, however. If one were looking for parallels the phrase in Isa 9:5/6, "Everlasting Father" (if that is a correct rendering of the 'ᵃbî 'ād would seem as probable, although there it is applied to the future Davidic king. It seems more natural, however, to see the phrase as one coined by the writer of the book of Daniel to stress the permanence of God's rule in contrast to the upstart "Little Horn," who is elsewhere said to have been granted a limited period of time only (9:25f.), elsewhere described again as "some days" (11:20,33). The description of the "Ancient of Days" closely resembles some features of the theophany described in Ezek 1:26-28, while the mention of "thrones" in the plural may echo earlier Old Testament concepts of the "Council of Heaven."

It is not possible here to do justice to the endlessly continuing debate concerning the identity of the "one like a son of man." However, certain broad characteristics occasionally get overlooked in some discussion. He is not pictured as a heavenly deliverer coming down from heaven. Rather he comes to the Ancient of Days and is presented to him. He receives the kingdom from God. This amply demonstrates a characteristic of God which was stressed in the earlier narratives, that he "removes kings and sets up kings" (2:21) and that he rules the kingdom of men "and gives it to whom he will" (4:25). It was also stressed in the narratives that God's rule is an everlasting kingdom (4:3,34; 6:26), and it is this kingly rule which is given to the one like a son of man (7:14). If, therefore, the one like a son of man is not a heavenly de-

---

[56]See H. Ringgren, *Israelite Religion*, trans. D. Green (London: 1966) 287-91.

[57]See e.g. J. A. Emerton, "The Origin of the Son of Man Imagery," *JTS* 9 (1958): 288; and, now, J. Day, *God's Conflict with the Dragon and the Sea* (Cambridge: 1985) 151-76.

liverer, Noth's view, that the "holy ones" or "saints of the Most High" are angels of the heavenly host, becomes less likely. The nearest to an "other-worldly" eschatological view to which one could come is LaCocque's suggestion that the "saints" are the ideal Israel in heaven of which the true Israel on earth is the counterpart.[58] The interpretation given in the chapter, whether integral to the original vision or not, would be nearer the mark when it sees the one like a son of man to be a representative figure of the people of God who now receive God's rule with its deliverance from oppression for all time, with all its consequences for their life and worship. Thus Delcor's view that the one like a son of man is meant to depict the kingdom of God in contrast to the bestial kingdoms of this world has much to commend it.[59] Perhaps something of the old idea of the king as the representative of the corporate body of the nation before God and God's vice-gerent among the people is present. Yet with this writer's collectivization of the role of the Servant, one can hardly say that any individual significance of the son of man figure is pressed.

In short, the material of the vision of chapter seven, as of the other visions, uses the same symbolic language and mythical concepts in its picture of "the End" as the Enthronement Psalms and earlier exilic and other prophecy. The border between the this-worldly and the other-worldly is as vague here as it is there, no more, no less. Unless scholars had made up their minds already that there is such a genre as "apocalyptic" and brought to it pre-programmed ideas of the characteristics which allegedly mark it off from "prophetic" literature, it is difficult to see what they could find special about the eschatology of the book of Daniel. It is surely time to heed John Barton's insistence that, while we may speak of "apocalypses," distinguished by their literary form and perhaps some greater immediacy of God's intervention in the historical process, the term "apocalyptic" is misleading.[60] It has outlived its welcome and its usefulness. It is time it were quietly dropped.

*******

It has not been the intention of this paper to try to identify every possible echo or "citation" of earlier scripture.[61] It has rather been to inquire into the influence on the book of more general biblical themes. If the understanding

---

[58] LaCocque, *Daniel*, 126-28.

[59] M. Delcor, "Les sources du chapitre VII de Daniel," *VT*, 18 (1968): 290-312.

[60] See J. Barton, *Oracles*, 201f.

[61] M. Fishbane finds a considerable number of such citations, especially in the later visions. *Biblical Interpretation*, 489-95.

of the use of earlier biblical material which we have suggested may be found in the book of Daniel is at all justified, the following conclusions emerge. Ideas concerning the nature and purpose of the Exile and of the hope of final deliverance from it, already implied in the earlier narratives, have been taken farther in the visions. This has proved the basic theme which binds narratives and visions together, suggesting that the writer of the visions was also the one responsible for the final form of the book. The idea of the Babylonian Exile is given theological, almost symbolic extension to cover the whole period from 586 to the second century B.C. It was divinely ordained as a means of cleansing and preparation for the emergence of a community delivered and redeemed by God. Prophecies relating to the end of that Exile and the final victory of God, with the establishment of his universal reign, are reinterpreted and related to the events of the Antiochean persecution. In the meanwhile the suffering of the faithful was a vital part of that process of preparation. It had vicarious value for the whole community in the manner of the Suffering Servant of Second Isaiah. They must meanwhile remain faithful for very soon this newly refined community will emerge from the oppression of foreign rulers, free to resume the cultic worship and way of life for which the Torah called in a newly consecrated sanctuary. Political messianism has been entirely replaced by thought of a people of God. In the book of Daniel the ideals and hopes of theocracy *and* eschatology merge completely.

It is an honor to dedicate this article to one who, in his commitment to making the Bible live to the people of God in his own day, has continued the living and on-going process which we have seen also engaged the writer of the book of Daniel.

# DOUBLE LITERARY EDITIONS OF BIBLICAL NARRATIVES AND REFLECTIONS ON DETERMINING THE FORM TO BE TRANSLATED

EUGENE ULRICH
UNIVERSITY OF NOTRE DAME
NOTRE DAME IN 46556

The issues—theological, religious, political, historical, textual, philological, hermeneutical, and so on— that require consideration and decision before attempting a translation of the Bible are numerous and of so many different types that even to attempt to list them and their subdivisions, much less discuss them, would consume too much space.

In this paper I wish to explore simply one aspect of Bible translation, an issue which plays an important role in Bible translation but is seldom discussed, at least as an issue and not just an ad hoc instance. I wish to explore the issue of double literary editions of biblical texts, in the hope of shedding some light on the criteria for determining which textual form of the biblical text should be selected for a translation of the Bible when there are two or more alternative forms.[1]

---

[1]Terminology is unfortunately inadequate. When I use "Bible" in this paper I am generally meaning, and focusing on, the Hebrew Bible, or Tanak, or the Old Testament, but on

The "problem," as I see it, can be introduced by quoting the following criterion for selecting the specific form of the text to be translated:

> For the Old Testament the Masoretic Text is used, that is the text established in the eighth/ninth centuries AD by Jewish scholars who fixed its letters and vowel signs, the text reproduced by most manuscripts. Only when this text presents insuperable difficulties have emendations or the versions of other Hebrew manuscripts or the ancient versions (notably the LXX and Syriac) been used. . . .[2]

The general "problem" I am addressing, then, is whether the Masoretic Text is too often and too monolithically chosen or assumed as "the biblical text" to be translated. In cases of individual words or phrases in the MT the usual provocation that draws attention to the problem is the existence of plausible variants in other textual witnesses. But the specific issue that I wish to explore is that of double literary editions of biblical texts, insofar as this phenomenon poses a difficulty for the a priori selection of any single text as the basis for a translation.

By double literary editions I mean a literary unit—a story, pericope, narrative, poem, book, and so forth—appearing in two (or more) parallel forms in our principal textual witnesses, which one author, major redactor, or major editor completed and which a subsequent redactor or editor intentionally changed to a sufficient extent that the resultant form should be called a revised edition of that text. The subsequent redactor or editor could, of course, be the same person who produced the original edition, as sometimes happens in literature, painting, music, or other art forms, but presumably the subsequent editor would be a different person.

Sometimes the scope of the pair of editions encompasses only a single story, narrative, chapter, or set of chapters. Sometimes the scope of the double edition extends to the entire biblical book, as in the case of Jeremiah. At the shorter end of the spectrum, if the scope of the variant tradition is smaller than a single pericope, then "literary edition" is too elevated a term and "textual variant," or "set of textual variants," is more appropriate. At the

---

none of these terms precisely with their particular connotations. That is, by "Hebrew Bible" I do not mean to exclude witnesses to the Hebrew text preserved only in Greek, Aramaic, Syriac, Latin, etc. Nor do I necessarily mean to exclude or include ancient Jewish writings in Greek which were considered sacred and authoritative but not accepted into the rabbinic canon. And though my attention is on Tanak or the Old Testament, I do not think that all my remarks will be unrelated to the principles underlying a translation of the New Testament.

[2]*The New Jerusalem Bible* (Garden City NY: Doubleday, 1985) xii. I am not singling out *The New Jerusalem Bible* for criticism; I randomly selected one of the many Bibles which sit on my shelf, and the introduction to the first Bible I picked up simply stated clearly and precisely the method that I think is at work, by reflective choice or by unreflective custom, as the principle underlying the work of many Bible translators.

longer end of the spectrum, one could consider the double edition of the Deuteronomistic History.[3]

For individual variants, the selection of a given reading in the MT, a Qumran manuscript, the LXX, or some other version usually does not have ramifications for the selection of variants in subsequent passages. For double literary editions of extended passages, however, unless a certain textual witness (for example, the MT) has been selected in principle as the single textual tradition to be translated throughout the whole Bible, then it may emerge that the study of double literary editions will logically require, if the MT has been selected for one passage, the selection of an alternate textual tradition for a subsequent passage. My hope is that analysis of this phenomenon will help illuminate the criteria by which Bible translators decide which form of the text is to be selected as ''the text'' to be translated as ''The Holy Bible.''

## DOUBLE LITERARY EDITIONS OF BIBLICAL NARRATIVES

One of the best among recent books to put into graduate students' hands in order to let them watch the process of integrating textual and literary studies is *The Story of David and Goliath: Textual and Literary Criticism: Papers of a Joint Research Venture* by Dominique Barthélemy, David W. Gooding, Johan Lust, and Emanuel Tov.[4]

The book lets us watch four different scholars with different backgrounds, training, and specializations present their initial solution to a problem, respectfully learn from and critique each others' solution, and then present another attempt at solution.

One of the results that emerge from the book, or rather, one of the facts which form the problematic for the book, is the double edition of the story of David and Goliath. Someone in antiquity took a traditional form of the story of David and Goliath and intentionally interspersed another account of Davidic traditions into it, thereby creating a significantly different edition of the text in quantity and in content. The book thus confronts those who attempt translations of the Bible with a problem—a problem of riches—the fact of double literary editions of biblical texts.

The editorial procedure of weaving into one narrative a quite different version of the same or a similar narrative is well known. That is exactly what happened, for example, in the Flood narrative with the versions commonly

---

[3]See, e. g., Richard D. Nelson, *The Double Redaction of the Deuteronomistic History* (*JSOTSup* 18; Sheffield: JSOT Press, 1981).

[4]D. Barthélemy, D. W. Gooding, J. Lust, and E. Tov, *The Story of David and Goliath: Textual and Literary Criticism: Papers of a Joint Research Venture* (*OBO* 73; Fribourg, Suisse: Editions Universitaires; Göttingen: Vandenhoeck und Ruprecht, 1986).

attributed to the Yahwist and the Priestly Edition. But from the translator's point of view that case is different because all major surviving witnesses to the text attest to the same composite secondary edition.

The David-Goliath story is a clear example of two different editions of a biblical narrative,[5] both attested in textual witnesses which in different eras have had long-standing and widespread claim as "the Bible." An earlier edition of the text with its own integrity and its own specific viewpoint is still found in the witnesses to the Old Greek (OG), and a second, later, developed edition is now found in the MT. The edition embedded in the MT has intentionally expanded the narrative with identifiably different types of material and different David-traditions.[6]

One can list further examples within Samuel where there appear evidences, not just of variant words or phrases within the text, but evidences of variant editions of portions of the book. For example, Professor Stanley Walters[7] has proposed that the story of Hannah, which has long been recognized as rich in textual variants, is not a single edition of the story with haphazard textual variants. He maintains that the variants form a pattern: that a portrait of Hannah is presented in the Masoretic Text in one light and that a different portrait of her is presented in an intentionally different and consistent light in the Septuagint. Since his was an oral report, forming part of a larger project destined for later publication, I will not give details here. But preliminarily I would agree with him. I think that in 1 Samuel 1-2, the Masoretic Text and the Septuagint may well present two different forms of the text, one intentionally different from the other, but each internally consistent.

In one sense, it does not matter whether the example of 1 Samuel 1-2 is verified as an instance of two intentionally different literary editions of that narrative, since literary and textual critics will probably continue to identify more examples of double literary editions. Thus, let us work on the hypothesis that 1 Samuel 1-2 is preserved in one edition in the MT and in another

---

[5]For the detailed characteristics of the two editions, see *The Story of David*. The detailed characteristics should not distract us here, nor should our judgment concerning the priority between the two editions (see the following note). It should also be pointed out for clarification that the issue here is not "earlier" or "later" in the origin of the traditions, but "earlier" or "later" in the redaction of the stories as they appear in the LXX and the MT.

[6]Here I clearly side with Tov and Lust and disagree with Barthélemy and Gooding. The correctness of either position, however, should not deflect us from the main point that there do exist double literary editions of the biblical text, because (a) all four agree that this is an example of double literary editions, and (b) even if this particular example should fail, other examples will swiftly take its place.

[7]Professor Walters gave an oral presentation entitled "Translating Samuel: Problems of the Text" to the Textual Basis for Bible Translation Group at the Society of Biblical Literature annual meeting in Boston on 7 December 1987.

edition in the LXX, and that one of these two editions was intentionally re-edited from the other.

Insofar as that hypothesis can be verified, the critical reader of Samuel is confronted with a problem. The features of the two intentionally different literary editions of 1 Samuel 1-2 are not at all the same as the features of the two intentionally different literary editions of 1 Samuel 17-18. That is, the ways in which the MT and the LXX differ from each other in the Hannah story are quite different from the ways the MT and the LXX differ in the David and Goliath story.[8]

For 1 Samuel 1-2 we find in the earlier edition (the MT, I would preliminarily suggest) a straightforward account with one portrait of Hannah. In the secondary edition (the LXX) we find the intentional and consistent reshaping of that account, arguably for theological motives and possibly for misogynous motives, to give a changed portrait of Hannah. When we turn to 1 Samuel 17-18, in the earlier edition (the LXX) we find a single version of the story, whereas in the secondary edition (the MT) we find a composite version: the same version as in the LXX, basically unchanged, but now augmented with inserted components of a second version quite different in content, details, and style.[9]

The Book of Samuel, of course, is not unique. If we look backward to the Torah, we quickly find other double editions, for example, in the Book of Exodus; and if we look forward to the Latter Prophets and the Writings, we find double editions also, for example, in Jeremiah and Daniel. These are not new findings, just samples that quickly come to mind. In each of these books we find intentionally variant editions of the text.

Let us focus first on the Book of Exodus. Here we meet a different type of intentionally different edition. Patrick Skehan published in 1955 a column from 4QpaleoExod[m] containing fragments from Exodus 32.[10] Initially he referred to the character of its text as being "in the Samaritan Recension," but subsequently he refined his assessment: the scroll "has proved on further study to contain all the expansions of the Samaritan form of Exodus, with one no-

---

[8]For the present we will not digress to the larger issue of the editing of Chronicles from the sources of Samuel-Kings.

[9]Even if Barthélemy and Gooding were correct, the point made here still holds: the rationale for the difference between the two literary editions of the Hannah story is different from the rationale for the difference between the two literary editions of the David-Goliath story.

[10]P. W. Skehan, "Exodus in the Samaritan Recension from Qumran," *JBL* 74 (1955): 435-40. In the early days the ms was designated 4QExod[α] and was sometimes confusingly cited as 4QExod[a].

table exception: it did not contain the addition to the Ten Commandments after Exod 20:17, referring to the unhewn altar on Mt. Gerizim."[11]

Thus, in 4QpaleoExod[m] we have a Jewish edition of Exodus. It displays a texttype of Exodus intentionally re-edited in conscious distinction from the Masoretic texttype. That re-edited texttype was subsequently taken over by the Samaritans, perhaps uncritically, that is, without reflection on the different available texttypes of Exodus and without a conscious decision to use this texttype as opposed to the different texttype also transmitted in Jewish circles and eventually used by the Masoretes. The Samaritans then inserted a single additional expansion, referring to the altar on Mt. Gerizim, according to the same method by which the expansions characteristic of the edition in 4QpaleoExod[m] were made.

But our focus here remains on the two Jewish texttypes of Exodus, the MT and 4QpaleoExod[m]. What we see in the revised edition of Exodus found at Qumran is different from what we discovered in either of the revised editions in the Samuel narratives. In the secondary edition of the text of Exodus we find neither an intentional reshaping of stories to give a changed emphasis or changed portrait (as in the Hannah story), nor an intentionally composite edition made by supplementing a single tradition with additional contents of sizable proportions from a quite different type of narrative (as in the David-Goliath story).[12] We find a text intentionally expanded by systematic harmonization[13]—by taking other parts of scripture and placing them virtually word-for-word in a new, related context, sometimes from nearby places in Exodus, sometimes from parallel passages in Deuteronomy. For the book of Exodus, the MT and the LXX preserve an earlier form of the text, whereas 4QpaleoExod[m] preserves a secondary edition of the text produced—still presumably by Jews—on the principle of harmonization. To complicate matters, the MT and the LXX may well exhibit different editions of Exod 35-40, but that we shall not explore here.

The two editions of the Book of Jeremiah have become widely known. 4QJer[b] and the LXX display a form of the story which Emanuel Tov[14] has

---

[11]P. W. Skehan, "Qumran and the Present State of Old Testament Text Studies: The Masoretic Text," *JBL* 78 (1959): 21-25, esp. 22. Judith E. Sanderson, who collaborated with me on the completion of Skehan's edition of that scroll for publication in a forthcoming volume of *Discoveries in the Judaean Desert*, has published an excellent analysis of the textual character of the scroll in *An Exodus Scroll from Qumran: 4QpaleoExod[m] and the Samaritan Tradition*, HSS 30 (Atlanta: Scholars Press, 1986).

[12]Lust (*The Story of David*, 13-14) characterizes the material of the earlier, shorter edition as "heroic epic" material, and the supplemental material as "romantic epic" material.

[13]Sanderson, *An Exodus Scroll*, 196-220.

[14]Tov ("Some Aspects of the Textual and Literary History of the Book of Jeremiah," *Le*

labelled "edition I," and the MT, 2QJer, 4QJer[a], and 4QJer[c] display a subsequent, intentionally expanded edition, "edition II." Tov has outlined very convincingly the characteristics by which edition II goes beyond edition I. There are both editorial aspects and exegetical aspects. Under editorial aspects Tov lists the rearrangement of text, the addition of headings to prophecies, the repetition of sections, and so forth. Under exegetical aspects, he lists the clarification of details in the context, the making explicit of material that was implicit, minor harmonistic additions, and the emphasizing of ideas found in other parts of the book.[15] Thus the two editions of Jeremiah exhibit yet another type of contrast. Here the scope of the secondary edition is the entire book, and the method is basically rearrangement plus expansion—expansion not by relatively infrequent, large-scale harmonization (as in 4QpaleoExod[m]) but by routine minor explicitation, clarification, lengthened forms of titles, and so on.

When we turn to the Book of Daniel, we find yet a fourth type of intentionally different editions in the biblical text. Though for most of the book the MT and the OG witness to the same edition, they exhibit two different editions of chapters 4-6. In chapters 4 and 6 the MT is considerably shorter than the OG, whereas in chapter 5 the OG is noticeably shorter than the MT. The least that can be said is that the same process is not consistently at work in these three chapters. But we can get much more specific. When we analyze the MT and the OG in parallel for each of the three chapters, the principal factors become clear. The differences in the quantity of text are not, as often in the MT of Samuel, caused by loss of sizable amounts of material through parablepsis. In Daniel 4-6 both the MT and the OG are apparently secondary, that is, they each expand in different directions beyond an earlier common edition which no longer survives. For example, for each of the three speeches in 5:10-12, 13-16, 17-23, the edition preserved in the MT greatly expands for rhetorical and dramatic effect beyond the edition preserved in the OG. The variant editions for chapter 4, in contrast, are signalled by the differing arrangements of various components and are confirmed by expansions in the OG, such as the expansion (perhaps a Babylonian astrological motif) of the

---

*livre de Jérémie: Le prophète et son milieu, les oracles et leur transmission*, BETL 54, ed. P.-M. Bogaert [Leuven: University Press, 1981] 145-67, esp. 146) correctly maintains that "the scroll resembles the LXX in the two major features in which the reconstructed *Vorlage* of that translation differs from the MT, namely, the arrangement of the text and its shortness as opposed to the longer text of MT. It should be remembered that the fragment is rather small, but the recognition of these two main characteristics in the fragment is beyond doubt." See also Tov's newer formulation in "The Literary History of the Book of Jeremiah in the Light of Its Textual History," *Empirical Models for Biblical Criticism*, ed., Jeffrey H. Tigay (Philadelphia: University of Pennsylvania, 1985) 213-37.

[15]"Some Aspects," 150-67.

sun and moon dwelling in the great tree (4:8), and so forth.[16] Thus, the double editions found in Daniel 4-6 are two different later editions of the story, both secondary, both expanding in different ways beyond a no-longer-extant form which lies behind both.

In summary, then, we have shown examples of four different books of the Bible with text forms preserving intentionally variant editions of the biblical text. For the Book of Exodus, the MT and the LXX preserve an earlier form of the text, whereas 4QpaleoExod^m (and subsequently the Samaritan text) preserves a secondary edition of the text produced on the principle of harmonization, spanning the majority of the book.

For the Books of Samuel, we have one clear example and another plausible example, offering two different types of intentionally new edition of individual narratives. On the one hand, in 1 Samuel 1-2 the MT may be the earlier form, and the text translated in the LXX may witness to a secondary edition with an intentionally altered portrait for theological motives. On the other, in 1 Samuel 17-18 there are clearly two intentionally different editions, the Greek now displaying the earlier edition and the MT a second edition supplemented by diverse David traditions.

For the Book of Jeremiah, the LXX displays an earlier edition of the entire book with one arrangement ("edition I") and the MT an expanded second edition ("edition II"), in substance basically unchanged, but with a variant arrangement and with systematic expansion by numerous, routine, minor additions.

For the Book of Daniel, the MT and the OG exhibit two different editions of chapters 4-6, this time both apparently being secondary, that is, expanding in different directions beyond an earlier common edition which no longer survives.

## WAS THE SECOND EDITION PRODUCED
## AT THE HEBREW STAGE OR BY A GREEK TRANSLATOR?

Before proceeding, it may be helpful to determine whether the second of the two different literary editions in each of the four biblical books discussed above was produced at the Hebrew stage or by a Greek translator. And I would like to preface our analysis with two observations.

First, with regard to the question of "theological *Tendenz*" or "actualizing exegesis" on the part of LXX translators, I have yet to examine an allegation of a major interpretative translation by an OG translator and be convinced that the OG translator was responsible for a substantively inno-

---

[16]See the forthcoming dissertation of Dean Wenthe analyzing this material in detail.

vative translation. Most who make such allegations have failed to distinguish the three stages of (i) the Hebrew *Vorlage* which is being translated into Greek, (ii) the results of the transformational process by the original Greek translator, and (iii) the subsequent transmission history within the Greek manuscript tradition.[17] In most cases the OG translators were attempting to produce a faithful, not innovative in content, translation of the sacred text.

Secondly, in contrast, it is methodologically important to examine the question for each instance, because it remains a possibility that, since the OG translators operated on partially differing applications of principles, a certain individual translator may turn out to have exercised substantively creative interpretation in the translation.

Examining now the four books we have just discussed, happily we find that the case is quite clear for the Book of Exodus: the second edition was produced at the Hebrew stage, for the two texts which contain the later edition, 4QpaleoExod[m] and the Samaritan, are both in Hebrew. And if confirmation be sought, the LXX of Exodus (at least up to chapter 35) is a faithful translation of a short, earlier Hebrew text very close to that in the MT.

In Samuel, for the David-Goliath story, Lust and Tov both considered the edition witnessed by the LXX as prior to that witnessed by the MT. And though both Barthélemy[18] and Gooding[19] began by leaving open the possibility that the secondary literary activity could have been at either the Hebrew or the Greek stage, at the end both were largely, if not fully, convinced that Tov was correct that the second literary edition had been made at the Hebrew stage.[20] For the Hannah story, Professor Walters was not yet prepared to say whether he thought one version was earlier than the other, perhaps wisely so, since I am not sure that I have yet posed precisely the correct question. But for my part, I think I have shown in general that many variants found in the OG of Samuel (including some in the Hannah story) are identical with variant Hebrew readings in 4QSam[a],[21] the bulk of those OG agreements with the Qum-

---

[17]One clear example of such allegation and its subsequent correction is F. F. Bruce, "The Oldest Greek Version of Daniel," *OTS* 20 (1975): 22-40, corrected by Sharon Pace, "The Stratigraphy of the Text of Daniel and the Question of Theological *Tendenz* in the Old Greek," *BIOSCS* 17 (1984): 15-35; see now more fully, Sharon Pace Jeansonne, *The Old Greek Translation of Daniel 7-12*, CBQMS 19 (Washington: Catholic Biblical Association, 1988).

[18]*The Story of David*, 54, but inaccurately summarized by Gooding, 56.

[19]Ibid., 83.

[20]Ibid., 138, 145.

[21]*The Qumran Text of Samuel and Josephus*, HSM 19 (Missoula MT: Scholars Press, 1978), esp. 40-41, 48-49, 71-72.

ran Hebrew surely being faithful translations of a Hebrew *Vorlage* in that text tradition.[22]

For the Book of Jeremiah, 4QJer[b] provides in Hebrew an exemplar of the shorter text tradition of which the LXX is a faithful translation, while 4QJer[a] and 4QJer[c] present Hebrew texts which agree with the secondary edition found in the MT.

For the Book of Daniel, the evidence is not yet conclusive, but it appears that the secondary editions were both made at the Aramaic level.[23] The MT and the OG seem to reflect the same edition through most of the book. Sharon Pace Jeansonne has demonstrated that the OG of 7-12 is a faithful translation of its Semitic *Vorlage*,[24] and the same seems true for chapters 1-2.[25] In chapters 4-6, however, we recall that the MT and the OG exhibit two different editions, this time both apparently being secondary, that is, expanding in different creative directions beyond an earlier common edition which no longer survives. But from the perspective of the OG as a single document, the OG of 4-6 appears to be woven from the same fabric as the OG translation of 1-2 and 7-12. Thus, the OG seems to be a consistent, unified document with a consistent translation technique. Therefore, the significant variation between the OG and the MT in 4-6 seems to indicate that the OG is a faithful translation of a different literary edition of these chapters. That would mean that again for Daniel the editorial activity resulting in secondary editions found in the MT and OG witnesses was done at the level of the original language. At the very least we can maintain that for the examples from Daniel 5 mentioned above the secondary literary activity was done at the Aramaic stage.

The point to bring out in our present discussion is that in a number of instances of double literary editions preserved in our textual witnesses, the secondary editorial work was already done at the Hebrew (or, for Daniel, Aramaic) level within the Jewish community and cannot be discounted as the unimportant or regrettable work of a Greek translator. The parallel editions were current, available forms of the biblical text in the original language, apparently with equally valid claims to being "the biblical text."

---

[22]We should also observe that the editing of Chronicles from the sources of Samuel-Kings took place at the Hebrew level.

[23]We will not even attempt here to bring up the question of the larger Book of Daniel with the "additions," further complicated by the appearance of that longer edition in the presumably Jewish recension, presumably based on a Hebrew-Aramaic *Vorlage*, attributed to Theodotion.

[24]*The Old Greek Translation of Daniel 7-12*.

[25]For the moment I suspend judgment on the unclear case of chapter 3.

## REFLECTIONS ON DETERMINING WHICH FORM
## OF THE BIBLICAL TEXT TO TRANSLATE

If it is true that there exist double literary editions of biblical books and passages in our preserved textual witnesses to the Bible, that these alternate editions were produced in Hebrew in the Jewish community prior to the emergence of Christianity, and that our evidence shows that until and somewhat beyond the fall of the Second Temple they shared equally valid claims to being "the biblical text," then Bible translators are faced with a question: how do we go about selecting the form of the text that should be translated?

When we ask that question, a large number of other questions immediately descend upon us, many fighting for first place. The preceding arguments have been largely in the scholarly, empirical arena; is that the starting point for deciding questions of Bible translation? How are the different arenas to be weighted? Upon what basis is the question to be decided: theological argument or empirical argument, denominational custom or ecumenical unity, and so on?

It is impossible to attempt to answer these questions properly in this short paper. The questions and considerations bearing on a Bible translation for religious or denominational purposes[26] eventually diverge widely from those bearing on a translation for scholarly or study purposes. In this paper, therefore, we can focus only on the latter, hoping that what is said is not entirely unrelated to the former. So I would like to focus on some of the criteria by which we determine which form of the text is to serve as the text to be translated for a "scholarly Bible." It is presumptuous to think that I can fully answer even this single question here. Rather, I offer some reflections—not considered as definitive but as one moment in an unfinished dialogue—that should be included among considerations of the issues of Bible translation. In fact, I am quite conscious that my reflections may end with more questions raised and left unanswered than questions answered. Perhaps, then, this can be read as a call for continuing and updated dialogue in light of our advancing knowledge and resources relative to the question of the textual basis for Bible translation.

We can begin by noting that it seems to be a defensible position (1) that different translations of the Bible can be produced as the result of legitimately differing scholarly judgments on historical or philological or other principles,

---

[26]Though for reasons of space the focus in this paper is restricted to the scholarly aspects, and cannot cover the theological or religious aspects of our topic, I want to say that I think there can be legitimate reasons within a religious community for choosing to translate a specific textual tradition.

(2) that different translations of the Bible can be produced as the result of legitimately differing theological positions or denominational needs, and (3) that both "scholarly Bibles" and "worship Bibles" have their place. The large number of recent translations would seem to corroborate this.

Since both in theory and in practice the MT is predominantly chosen, by conviction or otherwise, I think it important that we reflect on the basis for this choice. The specific issue I am trying to explore here is whether the optimum procedure for those who intend to produce a translation of the Bible based on scholarly principles is to use the MT as the textual basis except where that text is disturbed.[27]

For a scholarly Bible, either a specific text form must be selected a priori as the text to be translated, or parallel text forms must be examined throughout to determine which form is preferable as the basis of the translation. So that readers may know what kind of text they are dealing with, a decision should be made and announced in the introduction whether the translation is made from a particular ms or from a critically established text.

Should a specific text tradition be chosen a priori? Unless the goal is to produce a translation of the MT as a literary or religiously influential document, or to produce a translation of the LXX or another version as a literary or religiously influential document, then it would seem that the only reason for selecting a specific text form for a scholarly translation would be despair that a sufficiently solid basis can be found for a critically established text. An argument that usually accompanies this last position is that a diplomatic text, that is, the printing of the text found in a particular manuscript as opposed to a critically established or eclectic text, at least offers a text that actually existed and was used.[28]

A decision to translate the text form preserved in the MT can be made legitimately in principle (a priori), and can possibly—but subject to debate—be made as a result of examination of various text forms concluding that the MT is simply the best text (a posteriori).[29] A decision in principle to translate the MT specifically[30] is completely legitimate and desirable, on both schol-

---

[27]See, as an illustration, the quotation at p. 102n2 above.

[28]Though some find this a persuasive argument, I question its depth for several reasons. Here I will mention only one, noted by Tov ("The Text of the Old Testament," *The World of the Bible*, ed. A. S. van der Woude [Grand Rapids MI: Eerdmans, 1986] 156-90, esp. 157): "Except in the case of photographic reproductions of the same text, no two editions of the Hebrew Bible are identical." We can now include also electronic reproductions, but neither detracts from the point that Professor Tov makes.

[29]Even this idea of translating "the MT" is a highly complex issue; cf. M. Goshen-Gottstein, "The Textual Criticism of the Old Testament: Rise, Decline, Rebirth," *JBL* 102 (1983): 365-99.

[30]E. g., the recent translation by the Jewish Publication Society.

arly and religious grounds. The MT is a literary document with a magnificent history, and it has been highly influential and carefully protected; we should all have available a modern translation worthy of this religious and cultural treasure. And there can be no question that the modern Jewish community, even if it were to have alternate translations, should possess a translation of the specific text form of the MT which the Rabbis and the community have by conscious decision held sacred from antiquity. An analogous argument for a translation of the LXX can also be made.[31]

Most, however, appear to agree with the prevailing consensus that generally it is the "original" text that is to serve as the basis of translations; thus, if an a priori option for a specific text form were to be made, the MT would be the only viable candidate for that choice.

The MT does have the practical advantage of being a complete collection (unlike the Qumran scrolls) in Hebrew (unlike the versions) of texts of "the Hebrew Bible." Also, statistically it is probably true that a good, critical translation will in the main agree with the MT more than with any other single source. But it should also be kept in mind that "the Masoretic Text" is not a univocal term; it is a quite equivocal term. "The Masoretic Text" is not one text; it is a collection of texts—just as, for example, the LXX is—a collection of texts of divergent textual provenance, divergent stages of literary edition, divergent literary merit, divergent textual quality, divergent texttype, and so forth. For certain books, for example, Exodus, the MT proves to be the best single witness in general to the early text of the book.[32] For other books the case is different; for example, in Samuel, 4QSam[a] [b] [c] all prove to be superior in general to the MT,[33] though available only in very fragmentary condition, while the LXX proves to be superior in a large number of readings, though often resting on the basis of retroversion.[34]

But while agreeing that it is the "original" text that is generally to serve as the basis of translations, not all agree on the meaning of "original." My understanding of Jerome's position and the position of the translators in the

---

[31]E. g., Marguerite Harl's translation of the LXX as the Bible for Jewish and Christian readers in antiquity; cf. *BIOSCS* 13 (1980): 7-8, and *La Bible d'Alexandrie. La Genèse. Traduction et Annotation des Livres de la Septante* (Paris: Editions du Cerf, 1986).

[32]Cf. Sanderson's careful detailed analysis and assessment in *An Exodus Scroll*, 53-108, 307-311, esp. 309.

[33]For 4QSam[a] cf. Cross, "A New Qumrân Biblical Fragment Related to the Original Hebrew Underlying the Septuagint," *BASOR* 132 (1953): 15-26; and Ulrich, *The Qumran Text*. For 4QSam[b] cf. Cross, "The Oldest Manuscripts from Qumran," JBL 74 (1955): 147-72. For 4QSam[c] cf. Ulrich, "4QSam[c]: A Fragmentary Manuscript of 2 Samuel 14-15 from the Scribe of the *Serek Hay-yahad* (1QS)," *BASOR* 235 (1979): 1-25.

[34]Cf. E. Tov's judicious treatment of the problem of retroversion in *The Text-Critical Use of the Septuagint in Biblical Research*, Jerusalem Biblical Studies 3 (Jerusalem: Simor, 1981).

early Reformation period is that their eye was on the "original" in the sense of the Hebrew as the original language in which the texts were written. Is there any cause to doubt that the "*Hebraica veritas*" they sought was the Hebrew scriptures in their original language, which they, without distinct awareness of alternate Hebrew forms, happened to equate with the MT? Are there any indications that they chose the MT in contradistinction to alternate Hebrew text forms of whose existence they were aware but which they passed over?

We know Augustine's choice (!), but if Jerome or the translators in the early Reformation period had had Hebrew texts available like 4QpaleoExod$^m$, 4QSam$^a$, 1QIsa$^a$, and 4QJer$^b$ alongside "the Hebrew" they knew (namely, the MT), would they have chosen the MT? Here, of course, we can only speculate. But does it not surpass speculation to suggest that, like Origen, they would have compared the different texts and made some kind of choice on systematic principles? Thus, for example, if they thought that the shorter text (if sound) was usually preferable, would they not have chosen the shorter text in each case; if the longer, would they not have consistently chosen the longer; or if they thought that, as Jerome did for the Book of Daniel, the more "messianic" text was preferable, then would they not have consistently chosen the more "messianic" text where available; and so forth? Insofar as this assumption is correct, does it suggest that we should consider readjusting our perspective on the MT?

Let us for a moment allow our imaginations to indulge in a bit of fantasy. Let us imagine that we discovered scores or hundreds of ancient biblical manuscripts in Hebrew, similar to the Qumran scrolls, but all complete and intact. Or let us imagine that the roughly 170 biblical manuscripts from the Qumran caves were all complete and intact. If either were the case, should we still translate simply the MT except where its text seems disturbed? Or should we carefully collate and examine all the parallel texts to determine which form of the text, verse by verse and book by book, is preferable as the basis for our translation?

Reluctantly taking leave of the world of fantasy and returning to our real situation, we find that our current situation, though highly impoverished, is more similar than dissimilar to our fantasy situation. Though we do not have an abundance of complete manuscripts in the original language, we do have some poor but proud replacements in the fragmentary manuscripts from the Judaean wilderness and in the complete but once-removed or twice-removed versions—once-removed for the original translation, and twice-removed for versional manuscripts which have suffered in their transmission history and for the sub-versions.

An encouraging number of individuals and committees who set out to produce biblical translations do use the witness of available Hebrew manuscripts and the versions when pondering individual textual variants. But what happens when the variant is not an individual word or phrase protruding rebelliously in a verse or passage that is otherwise in textual harmony? What happens when the variant is a variant edition of a full literary unit?

The collection of literary texts that constitute the Hebrew Bible exists in a variety of conditions. One of those conditions which occurs intermittently is that of parallel editions in the different textual witnesses of a given passage. Again, the Masoretic collection of texts contains different types of literary editions of the biblical books; that is, the distinguishing features of the editions which happen to be embedded in the textual traditions preserved in the various books in the MT are inconsistent in the manner of their variation from the distinguishing features of the editions embedded in other textual witnesses. Consequently, the particular editions in the MT—depending upon the criteria adopted by a single translator, a translation committee, or the community—will sometimes be seen as superior to the editions preserved in other witnesses, sometimes as different but equally good, sometimes as inferior.

If, for purposes of specific illustration, we were to decide that the textual basis of our translation should be the earliest careful edition of a text produced by an author or major editor and preserved in our textual witnesses, then for Exodus we would in general select the MT-LXX tradition, bypassing the 4QpaleoExod$^m$-Samaritan tradition (though choosing for individual variant readings whichever of the various witnesses offers the best reading). For Jeremiah, in contrast, we would set aside the MT edition and translate the OG edition in general (though correcting the OG at specific points by means of the MT and other versions insofar as they exhibit superior readings within that edition). And though selecting the MT for the Hannah story in Samuel, we would still select the OG for the David-Goliath story later in the same book.

If, on the other hand, we were to decide that the textual basis of our translation should be the latest careful edition of a text accepted as authoritative by a community, then we would select the MT for the Book of Jeremiah and for the David and Goliath story. But we would pass over the MT to select the proto-Samaritan text form (that is, the Jewish text form, as in 4QpaleoExod$^m$, subsequently adopted and preserved by the Samaritans, but without the specifically Samaritan changes) for Exodus and Numbers. And though selecting the MT for the David-Goliath story, we would select the OG for the Hannah story earlier in the same book.

For Daniel 4-6 we would, on either the "earliest" or the "latest" principle, still lack a criterion for deciding which text form to use for translation. Both the OG and the MT display secondary, developed editions of the narratives; and as yet I do not see a way to decide in favor of either edition as "the final adopted edition" of Daniel.

CONCLUSION

It is legitimate and desirable to produce translations of specific textual traditions of the Bible, such as the MT and the LXX. But insofar as the purpose of a scholarly Bible translation is to produce a translation based on a critically established text, then I would argue that the method of procedure must be the full and systematic comparison of the major textual traditions—in both micro-contexts (verse-by-verse) and macro-contexts (each book or section as a whole). It is quite probable that the spectrum of classifications of textual variation will be so widely differentiated that a fully consistent policy is impossible. And it is quite probable that it will prove very difficult to decide in many cases into which category an individual variant fits. Nonetheless, there should still be a discussion of the principles by which the selection is to be made. And the principles should be spelled out, as is usually done, in the introduction, so that users can know in advance the principles of selection.

It seems clear now from the evidence of double literary editions of biblical passages, just as it has long been clear from the evidence of individual variants, that a translation of the Bible which claims to be made on scholarly principles must rest on a critically established text. Serious thought should be given to the types of data as have been briefly presented in the first and second parts of this paper and to consideration of the options sketchily presented in the third part. Presumably, consideration of the options will result in a reasoned and consistent approach to establishing that text. Just as there has probably never existed a perfect single written exemplar of "the biblical text," so too we will probably never produce a perfect single translation of "the biblical text." If we think otherwise, we need only wait until the next generation, or look more widely to broader sections of the believing community, to realize that we have not in fact produced a perfect translation. What we must strive for is the best that the human mind and human methods can produce within our particular culture and our own generation.